The Poignant Being

The Interplay of Vulnerability, Existence, and Meaning

PUBLISHED BY: Mamoon Jahan

Table of Contents

Preface

Life, in all its splendor and struggle, is a journey of becoming. It is a mosaic composed of moments, choices, and relationships that define who we are and who we aspire to be. Among these elements, there are anchors—forces so profound they transcend time and circumstance. Chief among these is the love of a mother, a force both elemental and eternal, shaping our lives in ways we often fail to grasp until much later. This book is an exploration of those forces, a reflection on the intricate tapestry of life woven with threads of love, sacrifice, ambition, and humanity's ceaseless striving for meaning. When I began writing, I did not set out with a grand plan or a specific audience in mind. What emerged instead was a collection of reflections, memories, and insights—a deeply personal exploration that touches on the universal. At its heart lies the story of motherhood, not as a singular experience but as a multifaceted phenomenon that transcends culture, time, and place. The mother is more than a nurturer; she is the first teacher, the sanctuary, and often the unsung hero. Yet, her role has also become a battleground, shaped and reshaped by societal expectations and the tides of progress. In honoring this role, we uncover truths about ourselves and the world we inhabit. This book is not merely about mothers, though. It is about the delicate web of relationships that define family: fathers, children, siblings, and the roles they all play. It is about the ways we hurt and heal each other, the sacrifices we make, and the burdens we carry. It is about how families can be both sanctuaries of love and arenas of conflict, teaching us resilience, empathy, and the complexities of human connection. These lessons, drawn from my own life, form the foundation of this work.

In my earliest years, I learned the profound influence of my mother. She was my refuge, my teacher, and my anchor in a world that often felt chaotic. Her strength was quiet but unwavering, her love unconditional but demanding. She expected us to rise to the challenges of life, to shoulder responsibility, and to honor the bonds of family. Yet, like all relationships, ours was not without its struggles. There were moments of misunderstanding, of pain and growth, and of learning to navigate the inevitable tensions between dependence and independence, tradition and progress. These reflections are not confined to the personal sphere. They open into larger questions about society and the human condition. Why do we create families? What purpose do they serve beyond the biological imperative? How do they shape our identities and values? And how do they evolve as societal norms shift, often in ways that challenge their very foundations? In exploring these questions, this book examines the tensions between individual desires and collective responsibilities, between progress and tradition, and between freedom and duty. As I wrote, I found myself returning to themes of love and sacrifice, not just within families but in the broader context of human relationships. Love is a force of creation, but it is also a force of challenge and change. It demands vulnerability and courage, asking us to transcend our selfish instincts to care for others. Sacrifice, often maligned or misunderstood in modern discourse, is a cornerstone of this love. It is through sacrifice that we grow, that we learn the meaning of commitment and the value of others. But sacrifice is not without cost. One of the recurring questions in this book is how to balance selflessness with self-preservation, how to give without losing oneself. In my mother, I saw a model of this balance, though not a perfect one. Her life was a testament to resilience and adaptability. She navigated the challenges of a blended family, the complexities of marriage, and the burdens of societal expectations with grace and determination. Yet, she also carried the scars of these struggles, scars that shaped her but never defined her. Her story, like so many others, is a reminder that strength is not the absence of pain but the ability to endure and grow through it.

This book also delves into the societal structures that influence our lives. It critiques the dehumanizing aspects of modernity, where the sacred bonds of family and community are often overshadowed by the demands of individualism and materialism. It questions the assumptions of progress, examining how technological and social changes impact our relationships and values. For instance, how does the rise of digital culture reshape our interactions, our sense of belonging, and our understanding of intimacy? How do shifting gender roles challenge traditional notions of family, and what new possibilities do they offer? In exploring these questions, the book does not seek to provide definitive answers. Instead, it invites readers to reflect on their own experiences, to question their assumptions, and to engage with the complexities of human life. It is a conversation, not a lecture, and its goal is to spark thought rather than impose conclusions. One of the central themes of this work is the duality of human nature—our capacity for both creation and destruction, for love and cruelty, for growth and regression. This duality is evident in the dynamics of family life, where moments of profound connection often coexist with conflict and misunderstanding. It is also evident in society at large, where the forces of progress and exploitation, unity and division, play out on a grand scale. By examining these dynamics, the book seeks to illuminate the choices we face and the responsibilities we bear as individuals and as members of a larger whole. In writing this book, I have drawn not only from my personal experiences but also from a broader engagement with history, philosophy, and culture. I have sought to situate my reflections within a larger context, to connect the particular with the universal. The result is a work that moves between the intimate and the expansive, weaving together personal narrative, social critique, and philosophical inquiry. One of the questions that has guided me throughout this journey is: What does it mean to live a meaningful life? This question, I believe, lies at the heart of the human experience. It is a question that each of us must answer for ourselves, but it is also a question that is deeply shaped by the people and circumstances that surround us. For me, the search for meaning has been closely tied to my relationships with my family, my reflections on love and responsibility, and my engagement with the world's complexities. In reflecting on these themes, I have come to see life as a series of paradoxes. We are at once individuals and members of a collective, free and bound, creators and inheritors. These paradoxes are not problems to be solved but realities to be embraced. They challenge us to think deeply, to act responsibly, and to live authentically.

I have learned much upon this wretched path, yet still, I remain a humble pupil—forever unfolding, forever yearning. It is not mere knowledge that I seek, but understanding of the human soul and the shadow it casts. This strange, contradictory species, man, he who stands upon the earth as if suspended between two realms, between the heavens and the mud—how absurd, yet how profound! In his essence, in his body, he is a creation of the highest order, a divine thought made flesh. Yet, despite this, he chooses—by his own will, with arrogance or perhaps ignorance—to disfigure himself, to make of himself something less than perfect. Consider it, then: we are not like the machines that require constant renovations, facelifts, or upgrades—our form endures. What, then, is this human? Strong and weak, exalted and humbled in one fleeting breath. A single blow to the head, a single crushing strike to the body, and he is no more— nothing more than dust, nothing more than a whisper.

He rises once, only to fall again, endlessly ensnared by his own foolishness, never truly learning, never truly understanding the gravity of his being. It is as if he does not know, does not comprehend that he is human, a creature caught in the storm of his own contradictions. And yet, even in this, my own folly mirrors the greater folly of mankind. I have always chosen to be respected rather than liked. Yes, in my arrogance, I sought respect as a shield, thinking it would spare me the folly of affection's transient nature. Respect, cold and unyielding, was the fortress I believed would offer me security. To be liked—ah, that would have been too much of a surrender, too much of an admission of weakness, as if the heart could truly stand to be loved without becoming fragile, without becoming a fool. But now, what do I find? Respect, I see, is no fortress at all, but a hollow, brittle thing, incapable of sheltering the soul from its own needs and contradictions. For in this, mankind's greatest folly persists: he cannot embrace kindness, honesty, or goodness without scorn. He cannot care for his fellow man without calling it weak, without mocking it as pathetic. To love is to be a fool, in his eyes—he who would rather clutch at his pride than open his heart. I, too, have made this mistake. I have clung to my pride, fearing to show myself vulnerable, fearing to be seen as weak. And so, the world spins on, caught in the madness of this endless contradiction, and I—oh, I—am left to wonder, what can be salvaged from this tragic, tragic species? What can be redeemed from the twisted wreckage of pride, scorn, and fear?

We rise and we fall, seeking something beyond ourselves, yet never truly understanding the nature of our own souls. Caught between sky and mud, between the divine and the wretched, we stumble, forever unable to reconcile the contradictions within us. And so, I ask—what, in the end, can be salvaged? What, indeed, is there to redeem from this endless struggle, this eternal madness of man?

Introduction

My journey began with a cascade of questions. Why do we love the way we do? What is the essence of family? How can we find meaning in an increasingly fragmented world? These questions weren't abstract or distant; they were deeply personal, born out of my own experiences, lessons, and struggles. Writing this book became my way of exploring these questions, not as an authority but as someone seeking clarity and understanding. As I reflect, I see my life as a tapestry woven with themes that connect us all. Each thread carries a story, a relationship, a challenge, or a revelation. My observations and experiences, though uniquely mine, are enriched by the broader societal and philosophical currents that shape us all. It all started during our school days when one of our teachers told us, "If you make books your friends, you'll see how you improve over time." At the time, I knew she was referring to academic books—the kind most of us found uninspiring, especially in a class where only a select few were genuinely interested in studying. Who could be drawn to books that had remained unchanged for decades?

One day, however, I stumbled upon Robin Sharma's Who Will Cry When You Die? That moment was a revelation. I discovered an entirely new world of books—ones that were deeply personal, thought-provoking, and transformative. It was the start of my reading journey, and it opened my eyes to the richness of literature beyond the dull confines of academics. As I ventured into this world, I found books that resonated with the questions that had long lingered in my mind. My life, much like the narratives I read, became a reflection of universal themes of love, family, and identity. At the center of this narrative is my mother, a force of unconditional love and sacrifice. Her presence in my life has been both a sanctuary and a challenge. Through her, I learned the paradoxical nature of love: its ability to nurture and demand in equal measure. Her love shaped me, demanded accountability, and instilled values that have guided me through life's complexities. But it also left me questioning how we honor such love in a world that often undervalues it. Growing up in a blended family, I experienced the intricacies of belonging, acceptance, and conflict. My family was a source of immense joy and deep struggle, a place where resilience and compromise were daily lessons. Misunderstandings arose, tensions flared, and yet, these moments forced me to confront my imperfections and limitations. My father, too, was a pivotal figure. A man of contradictions, his presence taught me about strength and responsibility, but also about the difficulty of reconciling personal ambition with familial duty. These reflections on my parents revealed not just who they were, but how their roles and relationships shaped me.

As I began to look beyond the personal, I saw how societal forces influence the way we live and connect. The rise of digital culture, for example, has transformed how we interact with each other. While it has created unprecedented opportunities for connection, it has also led to the erosion of deeper, more meaningful relationships. I found myself questioning how societal norms and expectations shape our choices and how we navigate these changes without losing ourselves. Throughout my life, growth has been a recurring theme. Whether through personal exploration, relationships, or unexpected challenges, each experience has carried its own lessons and opportunities for transformation. Growth isn't always linear or comfortable—it is often messy, painful, and unpredictable. Yet, it is through these moments of struggle and discovery that I have come to understand myself and the world around me more deeply. One of the most transformative moments came when I stumbled upon Robin Sharma's Who Will Cry When You Die?. That book opened my eyes to a world of learning and self-reflection I had never known, beyond the confines of academic textbooks. It marked the beginning of a journey of personal growth, fueled by curiosity and a desire to see life through new perspectives. What I learned is that growth doesn't just happen—it requires intention, resilience, and an openness to change. Modernity, with all its advancements, presents its own set of challenges. The pace of life has accelerated, leaving little room for reflection. Societal roles and expectations are in constant flux, disrupting traditional relationships while offering new opportunities for reinvention. I found myself asking: How do we balance progress with preservation? How do we navigate a world that often prioritizes convenience over connection? This constant tension between creation and destruction, between love and fear, is a fundamental aspect of the human experience. It is a duality we must navigate, both in our relationships and within ourselves. And yet, it is also what makes life so profoundly human. This book is, above all, a work of hope. It acknowledges life's imperfections but affirms the resilience of the human spirit. It calls us to embrace our responsibilities—to ourselves, our families, and our communities. By doing so, I believe we can create lives of greater meaning and purpose, honoring the sacrifices of those who came before us while inspiring those who come after.

Thank you for joining me on this exploration. May it inspire you to move forward with courage, compassion, and purpose.

Chapter 1

The Profound Mother

"The union of husband and wife is the very forge of civilization, where the strength of man meets the grace of woman, each one an essential force in the creation of the modern world. A woman, supported by the steadfastness of man, rises as a force to be reckoned with, a pillar of might and purpose. Yet when a man is upheld by the wisdom and spirit of a woman, he ascends beyond the mortal realm—his soul touched by the divine, his actions guided by the heavens themselves. In their mutual support, they transcend mere existence, and in their togetherness, they shape the future of all."

I fell from the stairs, and the world felt hostile. Where did I turn? To my mother. When misfortune knocked, I wept in her arms. When the rebuke of my father lashed at my soul, I sought her solace. In alienation, I shared my sorrows with her; in despair, her words were my refuge. Even in sleepless nights, her presence banished the darkness. Is it not curious how the child instinctively clings to the mother, as though she were the embodiment of all that is kind, safe, and eternal? The mother is the child's sanctuary—the first love, untainted and unconditional. In her love lies the purity of emotion unshackled by the chains of expectation or reciprocity. But in this purity, too, lies a dilemma—a question that echoes in the recesses of my mind: When I stand before my wife and call her my first love, will I not feel the weight of dishonesty pressing against my chest? My mother's love was primordial, a force that existed before I had the words to describe it. And if one day my mother were to ask, 'Whom do you love more—me or her?' What answer could I give? Perhaps I would whisper the paradox of my heart: 'Mother, when I am with my wife, she reminds me of you, and when I am with you, the world shrinks until only you remain.' Is this not the nature of love—to echo, to reflect, to multiply its forms? I recall sitting with my mother and sister, flipping through the photographs of our childhood. My mother, radiant and youthful, narrates the stories behind the frames—the people who held us as infants, the hands that captured the fleeting moments. I see her in her early career, tirelessly balancing work and motherhood. My sister and I, mere children then, would wait eagerly for her return, racing to her embrace as though it were a prize to be claimed. And oh, how jealousy consumed me! I guarded her affection jealously, denying my sister the nearness of her own mother. In hindsight, I smile at my cruelty, for it was born not of malice but of a desperate desire to possess what I believed was wholly mine. Even now, they remind me: 'Remember, you wouldn't let your sister near me.' And I laugh, though the laughter carries with it the weight of reflection.

In 2015, my family and I moved into a new apartment, marking a significant milestone in our lives. I cherish the memories of helping my mother in the kitchen, learning valuable life skills, and bonding with her. One evening, while we were preparing dinner, she shared some wise words with me: "Son, learn how to cook so you can take care of yourself when I'm no longer here." Her motivation for saying this was her concern about her aging, as she had married later in life.

I was a sensitive child, and my mother's words struck a chord deep within me. I couldn't bear the thought of losing her one day. The world without my mother seemed unbearable, and I felt a sense of responsibility to take care of her. Leaving them to old age homes is unthinkable. Even if they're bedridden, I'll be there to support and care for them, just as they did for me when I was helpless and unaware. This got me thinking: Why do couples have children? Having children is often misconceived as a selfless act, but in reality, it's often driven by personal desires. People have kids for various reasons, but ultimately, it's about what they hope to gain from the experience. For instance, some may want a reason to love or be loved, to strengthen their marriage, or to fulfill cultural or societal expectations. Others may want to start a family to satiate their biological clock, gain an identity, or join a community of parents. However, people rarely consider the potential challenges and responsibilities that come with raising a child. They often have an idealized notion of parenthood, which can be disconnected from reality. The harsh truths of parenting, such as financial constraints, decreased freedom, and emotional turmoil, are frequently overlooked. When deciding to have a child, people rarely think about the problems their child may face, such as being born with a disability, or the potential impact of their own mortality on their child's life. They also rarely consider the strain that raising a child can put on their marriage, or the potential consequences of depriving their child of a two-parent household.

And yet, despite the risks and challenges that our parents took on to raise us, many of us will abandon them in their old age, leaving them to fend for themselves in nursing homes. Your parents took a risk to bring you here without knowing the consequences, and now you'll leave them to face old age alone. How pathetic.

My mother is a wise and experienced woman, but she often struggled to share her stories with me, as she felt I was too young to handle the hardships she had faced. My father had nine children from a previous marriage, and I had only one sister from my mother. This complex family dynamic often made it challenging for my mother to open up about her past.
As I grew older, my mother began to share more about her life, including the challenges she faced as a wife and stepmother. She came from a poor background, and her father had been left to care for their large family after her uncles, who worked in urban areas, abandoned them. To make matters worse, her father lost an eye in a violent altercation sparked by one of her uncles.

Despite these hardships, my mother and her siblings worked hard to achieve success. She became a nurse, and it was during this time that my father met her and proposed. My mother had to adapt to a new family and environment, which was not always easy.

However, her transition was not without challenges. While some family members, including my uncles and father's cousins, accepted her, my half-siblings struggled to come to terms with her presence. This was partly due to the circumstances surrounding my father's marriage to my mother, as he was still married to his first wife when he married her. While it's understandable that my half-siblings found it difficult to accept my mother, it's also important to recognize that she wasn't responsible for my father's decisions.

In the early days, my mother faced significant difficulties. My father's income had to be split between raising his children from his previous marriage and supporting my mother. My half-siblings lived in a village home, while my mother and father lived in a rented house.

My mother shared with me the painful experience of losing her first child, a daughter named Iqra, who passed away after just one year. She then struggled to conceive again for two years, until my elder sister, also named Iqra, was born. I was born a year later. Around this time, my parents purchased an old house, which was a significant improvement from the rented house they had been living in. Although it took some time, my half-siblings eventually accepted my mother, except for my eldest brother, who continued to struggle with accepting her.

I still grin from ear to ear when I think about a hilarious conversation I had with my mom. You see, my dad would often take my sister and me on these awesome bike rides to our village. We'd spend hours playing with our cousins, and those afternoons were pure bliss.

One evening, curiosity got the better of me, and I asked my mom a question that would change everything. "Mom, I've noticed that all our aunts have husbands," I said, "but why doesn't our other aunt (my stepmother) have a husband? Is he dead?" My mom's expression changed, and she let out a sly smile. "Her husband is your father," she said, dropping the bombshell.

I was stunned. My jaw dropped, and all I could manage was a feeble "Ahh!" My mom burst into laughter at my reaction, and I couldn't help but join in. What was even more surprising was that I hadn't even realized I had a stepmother! It was a moment of pure innocence, and one that my mom and I still fondly recall to this day. Eventually, those financial struggles paid off with time. However, it wasn't just the financial struggles that my mother faced, but also the emotional toll of dealing with my father. My father is an impatient and ignorant man who has always had a strained relationship with my mother's side of the family. Despite their kindness and generosity, he would often curse them, fueled by his arrogant assumption that they were seeking financial gain from him.

As I entered puberty, our financial situation improved significantly due to my mother's wise investment decisions, particularly in real estate.

However, my father's arrogance grew in tandem with our prosperity. He began to believe that he was solely responsible for our success, and that he had "put my mother on a pedestal."

In February 2021, my father underwent heart surgery. Thankfully, the operation was successful, and my mother and I waited anxiously in the waiting area while he recovered in the ICU. During that emotional moment, I saw my mother break down in tears. She revealed to me that she had prayed for my father's recovery, not for his sake, but for ours. She feared that if he were no longer around, my sister and I would be vulnerable to exploitation by our paternal relatives. Whatever grievances I hold against your father, I couldn't forget them, she said. However, my mother reminded me that he is a great father in many ways. He was indeed a generous soul. He would often take us to his office, where we had the freedom to do as we pleased. Our father always ensured that we had everything we needed at our fingertips. However, despite his many wonderful qualities, he was not perfect and had his flaws – a reminder that even the most well-intentioned individuals cannot be multiplied by zero, implying that everyone has their limitations and imperfections. Despite his flaws, his presence in our lives matters, and my mother wants us to appreciate him until we grow up and become successful.

The role of a mother in a child's life is undoubtedly significant. My mother has always been keen on instilling in us a strong sense of responsibility and self-sufficiency. Rather than hiring a maid to handle household chores, she encourages us to take ownership of these tasks, believing that they offer valuable learning opportunities and hands-on experience. For instance, on weekends, we work together as a team to tackle the laundry. My mother efficiently loads the washing machine, my sister expertly dries the clothes in the dryer, and I take charge of hanging them out to dry on the clothesline. This collaborative effort not only teaches us essential life skills but also fosters a sense of camaraderie and shared responsibility. I'm widely recognized for my good character, both within my family and in the various communities I've been a part of. Those who know me hold my character in high regard, and I attribute this entirely to my mother's outstanding guidance and influence.

Despite her professional commitments, my mother never compromised on loving, teaching, and caring for our family. Her kindness and generosity, however, extend far beyond our household. There is always this quality about her; she is always living for others, making sure she includes everyone in her prayers. She also selflessly reaches out to those in need, embodying the values of compassion and empathy that she has instilled in me. Through my own exploration and self-discovery, I've come to understand the complexities of human nature, including the darker aspects of human motives. However, it's been my mother's guidance and wisdom that have helped me balance this knowledge with empathy and compassion, allowing me to see the world from other people's perspectives and cultivate kindness and understanding. Her greatest triumph is rising above the negativity that once surrounded her, earning her the respect and admiration of both sides of our family.

As a nurse, my mother's medical expertise is sought after, even by her colleagues and superiors. Her struggles have paid off, and she's earned a reputation for being a compassionate and knowledgeable professional. In a world driven by pop culture, my mother remains humble and genuine. Her integrity is unwavering, and she's a shining example of a strong, virtuous woman.

I've always admired my mother's beauty, both inner and outer. However, I'm aware that not everyone is fortunate enough to have a mother like mine.

Ah, the modern world—a stage of decay and contradiction, where the next generation is birthed into a world of chaos, led astray by the hollow promises of convenience and fleeting ideals. The children of today—Gen Z, Gen Alpha, and whatever titles the future will bestow upon them—are being forged in an era devoid of heroes, where their role models are but shadows, and their villains are mere reflections of their own unacknowledged desires. Each life is unique, yes, but where are the values, the towering figures to inspire? The heroes of old have been replaced by the temptations of mediocrity, and the ideals of greatness have been supplanted by the trivialities of digital distractions. And yet, among this tide of confusion, there is one role that has been particularly defiled, one which once stood as the pinnacle of dignity—the role of woman. Mother, sister, wife—these titles, once sacred, are now undermined, belittled in the name of progress, of equality, of individualism. The woman who once shaped the very essence of life through her creation, her nurturing, her devotion, is now reduced to a mere cog in the machine of modernity. How tragic it is to see the grandeur of her role fade into the background, overshadowed by the frenetic pursuit of status and self. Do not mistake me—I do not deny the inherent dignity of the woman. When I speak of equality, I speak not of the hollow, superficial equality of labels and quotas, but of a deeper, more profound truth: the equality of human dignity, the recognition of the soul in its purest form. In matters of dignity, men and women are equal—each is endowed with the same capacity for greatness, for destruction, for creation. It is not the gender that defines their worth but the depth of their will, the force with which they shape the world. To reduce the woman to a mere reflection of modern ideals is to rob her of her true essence, to force her into a mold that does not honor the greatness of her potential. The modern world, in its misguided attempt to liberate, has enslaved the very soul of what it means to be human. If we are to rise, if we are to truly honor the dignity of both man and woman, we must look beyond the false idols of equality and return to the depths of what it means to be human, to truly embrace the roles that define us—roles not born of oppression, but of creation and profound purpose.

I recall a personal anecdote shared by one of our religious teachers. He had been married for twenty years, a long passage of time in the human condition, and one day, his wife—faithful as the very soil from which life springs—brought him breakfast in bed. A gesture both simple and profound. "You always cook for me," he remarked, "perhaps someday I should do it for you." And what did she respond with? Not gratitude, nor the acceptance of his patriarchal pity, but a mirror to his own life of hollow gestures. "Then perhaps," she said, "I should earn a living as you do, and provide for us as you do."

How satisfying, how fitting—her words pierced through the veil of complacency, reminding him that roles are not exchanged so easily, that the dance of power and submission cannot be so neatly folded into equal boxes. It is not the act itself that matters, but the undercurrent of expectation, the unspoken debt each partner feels toward the other. Yes, she too plays her part—her life bound by the same chains, but in truth, both play the role of the one who gives and the one who takes. And yet, to take is not always to receive, and to give is not always to offer.

And there, in the silence that followed her words, I found the answer satisfying, increasing my morale, Teacher said.

It is not a question of comparing rights, as if we are all merely equals in the eyes of a shallow and blind equality. No, it is a matter of respecting the roles that each plays, the unique forces that shape them, and the distinct paths they must tread. Women, like men, should be free to forge their own destinies, to conquer the realms of medicine, law, education, or any field where their will and ambition lead them. There is no inherent limitation to their capacity; their greatness is not bound by tradition but by the strength of their spirit. Let them pursue their passions without the yoke of prescribed gender roles, unbound by the constraints of what has been deemed "appropriate" or "expected." The path of each individual—man or woman—is their own to create. If a woman can deliver value, the same value as a man, in whatever endeavor she chooses, then the world must bend to the truth of that value. Equal pay, then, is not a concession, nor a bargain, but a simple recognition of the fundamental laws of worth. It should flow freely, as naturally as the exchange of energy in the world. But beware! This is not a plea for pity or special treatment. It is not a call to soften the world, to dull its edge with the false balm of equal opportunity where none is earned. It is a call to honor the power of women to rise, to challenge, to succeed—not as a reaction to the demands of others, but as a manifestation of their own will to power. If they can stand alongside men, shoulder to shoulder, and prove their worth, then let the world bow in recognition. But let no one forget—equality is earned through action, not through demand. It is through greatness, not entitlement, that true respect is given.

At times, I cannot help but feel a pang of envy at the reverence bestowed upon women in this society, a reverence that verges on the absurd. In this land of prescribed virtues, where dignity and chastity are exalted, women are placed upon a pedestal. They are granted privileges, such as being allowed to bypass men in lines, to receive their due not through effort but through an arbitrary decree of value. Yes, this is a society that claims to honor the woman, to raise her up as a symbol of purity and esteem. And yet, there is a grotesque irony beneath this veneer of respect. For all the exalted language, the false sanctity of her place, there is one domain where her autonomy is cast aside—the realm of choice in love. In matters of marriage, society acts as a jailer, confining her to the will of others, shackling her to the demands of tradition and convention. How can this society that lauds her dignity turn a blind eye when it comes to her right to choose a life partner? Let us speak the truth. It is women who will spend their lives in the home of another, navigating the labyrinthine currents of someone else's world. It is they who will bear the weight of unfamiliar dynamics, of challenges that may be unforeseen, their fate forever bound to the choices they make—or, worse, to the choices made for them. How then, can the hand that binds her in all else, deny her the right to choose the one with whom she will share her life? It is not mere justice; it is the primal law of existence that each must claim their own destiny. And in matters of love, as in all things, a woman must have the autonomy to shape her own path. The illusion of respect is worthless unless it grants her the true power to decide for herself—to choose, to act, to live. For it is in her choice, in her will, that her true dignity lies—not in the hollow rituals of deference, but in the power to claim her own life, to shape it as she wills.

Mother Instincts

Behold, the infection of Western culture that now seeps into our society like a poison, corrupting the very essence of what it means to be a woman, to be a person with purpose. These young women, once heralded as the honor of their families, are willingly tearing themselves asunder, chasing after ephemeral dreams spun on the webs of social media. They are seduced by the glittering stories of women who have amassed wealth and power, believing that such hollow victories will grant them the meaning they so desperately seek. Yet, in their blind pursuit, they fail to see the abyss at their feet—the dark consequence of their recklessness. These women, the supposed paragons of modern success, are often exploited without their knowledge, led astray by the false promises of independence and freedom. They are afraid to commit, afraid to surrender themselves to a partner, fearing that the act of love, of family, might shackle them and rob them of the precious pursuit of wealth and status. They have been conditioned to believe that they must sacrifice their womanhood for their career, as if the two can never coexist.

But as the years slip by, these high-achieving women—driven by ambition but hollowed by it—find themselves caught in a cruel irony. The clock ticks louder as they approach the barren land of the late thirties, where their once vibrant potential begins to be dismissed as "old and used." They reach a moment of reckoning, a jarring awakening, where the hollow pursuit of success, the ceaseless grind of professional accomplishment, no longer satisfies them. They stop, for the first time, to question: What have I truly achieved? What have I sacrificed? The world that they have built, one of endless striving, now reveals its emptiness. They realize that there is more to life than climbing the ladders of career success—more than wealth, more than titles, more than the hollow applause of society. The whispers of their biological clocks become the drumbeats of their soul, urging them toward a new creation: the creation of life, of family, of something beyond the self. These women, once driven by the tyranny of their own ambition, now seek balance—an alignment of their desires with their inner truth. Studies such as Pamela Stone's "The Opt-Out Revolution" and Catherine Hakim's "Women's Careers and Family Formation" have revealed a profound truth about the modern woman: that career choices, so long held as sacred, are often subjugated by a deeper yearning for personal fulfillment, for a sense of wholeness that cannot be found in the boardroom. This is the moment, the reckoning, that will define their legacy. They no longer chase success in isolation but seek a new definition of achievement—a life that honors both their professional aspirations and their inherent need to nurture, to create, to love. The question, then, is no longer one of career versus family, but of the possibility of integrating the two into a singular, authentic existence. What is success, after all, if it leads one to the ruin of the soul?

As I contemplate the state of motherhood in this era, a disquieting thought emerges: are we witnessing the decline of a sacred ideal? The traditional values of motherhood, once revered as the cornerstone of life itself, now seem to dissolve like shadows at dawn. My generation stands as a bridge, perhaps the last to carry forth these timeless virtues, while the younger generation stumbles under the weight of modernity, their hands filled with the empty trinkets of technology and fleeting trends. In this age of ceaseless noise, where every moment is mediated by a glowing screen, can the essence of motherhood survive? Or will it wither, cast aside as an artifact of a simpler time? I fear that the rising tide of Generation Alpha, with its allegiance to algorithms and ephemeral connections, may not inherit the profound truths that define motherhood. Yet, even as this fear gnaws at the edges of my thoughts, I am reminded of an eternal truth: the essence of motherhood is indomitable. Like the fire that warms the hearth, it is not bound by the structure of its surroundings; it exists beyond the contingencies of tradition or circumstance. Unconditional love, care, and nurturing are not mere customs—they are the pulse of life itself, the eternal song that resonates across the ages. Reflecting on my own life, on the love and devotion of my mother, I see that motherhood has always been a force of transformation. It adapts, it evolves, but it never loses its essence. The selflessness, the sacrifice, the unwavering presence—these are not inventions of any one age but are etched into the fabric of existence.

This thought offers solace: though the world may change, though we may lose the language to name it, the essence of motherhood endures. It is a primal force, immune to the fickle whims of culture. It is the eternal affirmation of life, the quiet yet unyielding defiance against chaos and despair. Even as the world around us grows alien and unfamiliar, the heart of motherhood remains. It will endure, for it is not merely a human construct but a reflection of the deeper truths of existence—a testament to the sacred in the mundane. And in this, I find hope: though the forms may change, the spirit of motherhood will forever remain.

The Role of Men

The role of men in perpetuating exploitation is a shadow that darkens the foundation of our age, a testament to the depths of human will when stripped of empathy and tempered by entitlement. Men, as architects of platforms that prey upon the vulnerable, have honed their craft with precision, wielding power not as creators of virtue but as merchants of gratification. These platforms, these temples of vice, are not accidents but monuments to the cultural disease that defines modern masculinity: the will to dominate masked as the pursuit of pleasure. Observe the younger women, drawn irresistibly to the narcissistic psychopaths of this era. These men—charming, charismatic, and confident—are predators cloaked in the allure of gods. Yet beneath their polished façades lies a labyrinth of manipulation and control, a machinery of the spirit designed to ensnare and consume. And why do these women fall? Why are they drawn to such destructive idols? It is the deep wound of validation they seek, a balm for scars left by emotional unavailability, by the haunting specter of past rejections, or by the gnawing despair of self-doubt. The narcissist, with his initial idealization, becomes not merely a lover but a savior—a false god offering salvation at the price of freedom. And once within his grasp, they are bound not by love but by trauma, shackled by the chains of a bond forged in pain. Childhood traumas, insecure attachments, the silent conditioning to prioritize others over oneself—these are not weaknesses but inherited burdens, thrust upon women by a culture that venerates sacrifice yet despises the sacrificial. These same forces craft a landscape where people-pleasing becomes a survival instinct, leaving many unable to see the trap until it is too late. Yet society does not stand idly by; no, it conspires in this tragedy. Through its stories, its art, its myths, it exalts the narcissistic psychopath as the brooding hero, the Byronic figure whose intensity is mistaken for passion, whose dominance is cloaked in the guise of romance. Romantic comedies, dramas, and the endless stream of media content distort love, turning poison into nectar and chaos into intimacy. What madness is this, that we revere those who destroy the very bonds they claim to sanctify? And what of social media, the ultimate instrument of objectification? Here, men do not merely exploit; they perform their cruelty for the world to see, creating and sharing content that reduces women to commodities. This is not a hidden shame but a celebrated ritual, a spectacle without consequence. And in its normalization, we find not just acceptance but encouragement, a cultural sanctioning of exploitation as entertainment.

Furthermore, the veil of anonymity granted by the digital realm has become a mask for cowardice. Behind the screen, men indulge their basest instincts, emboldened by the knowledge that they may escape accountability. This detachment from consequence, this freedom from the gaze of the other, corrupts the soul and turns man into both tyrant and wraith. Dostoevsky's words haunt us: *"Every man is not only responsible for what he does but for what everyone else does."* Is this the height of profundity, or is it madness? Responsibility is not a solitary burden but a shared creation. The world is not a mirror reflecting only our own deeds but a mosaic of countless choices, each contributing to the structure of reality. What you do, what you condone, what you ignore—all of this shapes the world you inhabit. To ask whether the consequences you reap are proportionate to your actions is to misunderstand: you co-create the world through your participation in it, shaped by the systems that surround you and the choices you make within them. But how, then, does one navigate this shared responsibility? When man and woman meet, how can they honor both their own nature and the dignity of the other? Consider this: a woman, walking her path, should feel empowered to remain steadfast, unbothered, and modest in her demeanor. Modesty is not submission but a declaration of self-respect—a shield that guards her dignity while amplifying her confidence. And the man? His task is no less demanding. He must demonstrate the strength of his character through restraint, by lowering his gaze and tempering his impulses. To avert the eye is not weakness but power—the power to acknowledge boundaries and to reject the tyranny of unchecked desire. In this simple act lies a profound truth: a true man is not one who commands fear but one in whose presence a woman feels safe, respected, and valued. But let us abandon the naive delusion that men and women can exist as mere friends without complication. This is not wisdom but self-deceit, a betrayal of the reality of human nature. Where attraction and desire simmer beneath the surface, to deny them is folly. Friendship between man and woman often becomes the stage upon which unspoken tensions play out, hidden beneath masks of civility. The path forward is neither denial nor indulgence but a recognition of the inherent dynamics at play. Respect, restraint, and the courage to confront the truth—these are the pillars upon which a balanced relationship must stand. Without them, we stumble into chaos, blind to the forces we ourselves have unleashed.

Throughout the annals of history, there have been moments—brief, flickering—when women's rights emerged, standing like lone beacons in the vast darkness of subjugation. In ancient Egypt, women wielded influence, owning property and participating in trade. In Sparta, they stood as equals in strength, with freedoms that surpassed those of their sisters in Athens. The Viking Age, too, granted women rights—property, divorce, power. Pre-colonial African societies and the early days of Islam afforded protections under law, recognizing the dignity of women within their cultural frameworks. Yet these were exceptions, not rules, and their coexistence with objectification reveals an eternal truth: empowerment and exploitation often walk hand in hand, one feeding upon the other. And now, history repeats its cruel symphony. Where once women fought for the acknowledgment of their humanity, they are again reduced to objects—marketed, consumed, discarded. Progress, we call it, as though the cycle has been broken. But it is not progress; it is the eternal return of exploitation, dressed in modern garb. The question is not whether men or women are more culpable in this downfall, but whether we can see the chains we have forged for ourselves. The objectification of humanity is no longer confined to women, though society's judgment falls upon them with greater weight. To be labeled "unchaste" or "immodest" is a scarlet brand, a public condemnation that speaks not to the individual but to a collective hypocrisy. Men, too, are objectified—though their chains are lighter, their punishment less severe. Yet in this shared degradation, neither gender is spared the tragedy of their own participation. What folly, then, is that in an age of boundless information—an age where wisdom is but a click away—women continue to make choices that harm their well-being, that compromise their essence. Is it ignorance? No, for ignorance cannot survive in the flood of light that saturates the modern world. It is something deeper, a willful blindness born of despair, of cultural forces that compel individuals to betray themselves in the name of fleeting validation. But the solution is not the pursuit of self-destruction disguised as freedom. True freedom lies not in surrendering to the forces of exploitation but in rising above them. Both men and women must awaken to their shared responsibility in this grand tragedy. For in the pursuit of equal rights, the chains of objectification are not broken—they are reforged, distributed anew, and fastened tightly. To break free requires not only awareness but the courage to reject the systems that profit from our downfall. The lesson of history is not that progress is inevitable but that it is fragile, easily co-opted, easily lost. To reclaim it, we must first reclaim ourselves, casting off the illusions that bind us and embracing the harsh truths that set us free. Anything less is not freedom but slavery by another name.

Take a moment to review the case studies provided below.

A study conducted by David M. Buss and Cindy M. Meston in 2017 explored the mate preferences of American adults. The study surveyed 1,000 adults aged 18-35 and found that 42% of men preferred a partner with some sexual experience, while 31% preferred a partner who was a virgin. In contrast, 27% of men had no preference. Women's preferences differed slightly, with 54% preferring a partner with some sexual experience, 21% preferring a virgin, and 25% having no preference.

A 2019 study published in the journal "Evolutionary Psychological Science" and conducted by Todd K. Shackelford also investigated mate preferences and sexual experience. The study surveyed 2,000 American adults aged 18-40 and found similar results. 45% of men preferred a partner with some sexual experience, while 29% preferred a partner who was a virgin. 26% of men had no preference. Among women, 51% preferred a partner with some sexual experience, 24% preferred a virgin, and 25% had no preference.

A 2019 study by the General Social Survey revealed intriguing insights into the sexual behaviors of Americans before marriage. On average, men reported having approximately 6.3 sexual partners, while women reported around 4.2 partners. Interestingly, the research also uncovered generational differences, with younger generations (born between 1981 and 1996) reporting more sexual partners, averaging 7.2 for men and 4.8 for women. Conversely, older generations (born between 1943 and 1960) reported fewer partners, with averages of 2.2 for men and 1.5 for women. Furthermore, regional variations emerged, with individuals from the Northeast and West Coast reporting more partners than those from the South and Midwest.

The studies on mate preferences and sexual experience highlight the changing values and attitudes towards relationships and intimacy. While some people prioritize physical pleasure over emotional connection, others seek a deeper and more meaningful relationship.

How disheartening it is to witness this peculiar modern desire—a preference for partners with prior sexual experience. The sacred, once reserved for one's soul mate, has been sullied, traded like a commodity in the marketplace of desire. What was once a bond of profound intimacy has become a transaction, weighed and measured by the calculus of experience.

But let us not stop at condemnation; let us understand. Consider the journey of self-discovery that begins in the fires of youth. During puberty, the stirrings of attraction emerge, raw and untempered. Yet society, with its financial chains and moral restrictions, bars the young from pursuing the permanence of union. What follows is a restless seeking, an exploration of desire in fragmented, fleeting encounters. And from this arises the preference for "experience"—a misplaced belief that only the seasoned can satisfy, that wisdom is earned through indulgence rather than restraint. Yet, how hollow this preference appears upon closer scrutiny! The inexperienced are not lesser for their purity, nor are the experienced greater for their indulgence. These preferences reflect not the truth of human nature but the distortion wrought by a world obsessed with gratification. To seek experience in a partner is to confuse skill with connection, surface with depth. And yet, personal preferences are but reflections of the inner chaos within us. Some seek familiarity; others, novelty. But beneath these preferences lies a universal truth: compatibility and mutual respect are the bedrock of any true union. To transcend the superficial, to forge a bond that elevates rather than diminishes—this is the rare alchemy of love. Here, we glimpse the profound: the Michelangelo Effect, that sublime phenomenon where relationships become a crucible for transformation. "I saw the angel in the marble and carved it until I set him free," said the great sculptor. And so it is with love. A true partner is not a critic but a sculptor, one who sees the beauty buried within the marble of the soul and works tirelessly to reveal it. Through encouragement, through support, through the forging fires of constructive challenge, the individual grows, not toward another but toward their ideal self. But this, too, is a rarity. For most relationships are not sculptors' workshops but arenas of consumption—partners devouring one another, mistaking satisfaction for growth, and desire for transcendence. To elevate love to the level of art requires courage: the courage to reject what society deems desirable and to seek instead what the spirit knows to be true. Love, like art, demands patience, discipline, and vision. Without these, it is not love but merely the hollow echo of a world that has forgotten its own depths. To truly love is to sculpt, and to sculpt is to liberate—not the partner alone, but oneself as well.

As I stand at the precipice of marriage, I am seized by a conviction that burns with clarity: the importance of marrying a virgin. This belief, far from being rooted in mere physicality, delves into the profound depths of the emotional and the psychological. It is not the unbroken seal of the body that captivates me but the unblemished sanctity of the shared journey—a union unmarred by the ghosts of past entanglements. To preserve one's virginity until marriage is to guard not only the body but the soul, shielding it from the detritus of fleeting desires and fractured connections. Such a choice is an act of defiance in a world that worships at the altar of gratification. It is a declaration of trust and loyalty, a bond forged in the fires of restraint and the purity of intention. What greater gift could there be than to offer one's uncharted self, to embark together on the unmarked terrain of intimacy, where every touch is discovery and every glance is revelation? Yet, look at the world around us—a world that has traded its soul for momentary pleasure, that prioritizes sensation over substance, and fleeting encounters over enduring connections. It is as if society has chosen to revisit a film already seen by countless others, content with reruns rather than the raw thrill of a first experience. What is lost in this exchange is not merely novelty but the profound joy of shared discovery, the sacred bond forged in mutual exploration. Today's society is besieged by fantasies spun from the threads of indulgence, a deluge of explicit content that corrodes the spirit and blurs the lines between desire and fulfillment. The values that once upheld restraint as a virtue are now mocked as relics of an outdated morality. And yet, in this so-called progress, we see only decay—a loss of the sacred, a descent into the profane. To marry a virgin, then, is not merely a personal choice but a rebellion against the tide of mediocrity that seeks to erode the essence of human connection. It is a testament to shared values, a mutual act of devotion that resists the call of the hollow and the ephemeral. For in this act lies a deeper truth: that love, like art, is most sublime when untainted by the banalities of the world. To choose the path of restraint is to choose the path of greatness, to reject the mire of modernity and instead ascend to a higher plane of existence. It is to say, "I will not be consumed by the fleeting; I will instead create the eternal." For in love, as in life, the only true beauty lies in that which endures.

Chapter 2

The Termites

"People talk sometimes of bestial cruelty, but that's a great injustice and insult to the beasts; a beast can never be so cruel as a human being, so artistically, so picturesquely cruel."

~ Fyodor Dostoevsky

Humans are a uniquely terrifying species, not because we are the strongest, fastest, or largest animals in the animal kingdom, but because of the unparalleled traits that make us effective hunters, relentless survivors, and, in many cases, the ultimate apex predator. At first glance, one might attribute this to our intelligence—and it's true that our brains play a significant role—but the horror of human nature and capability runs far deeper. It's a blend of physiological, psychological, and behavioral traits that have made us one of the most formidable forces in history. Consider ancient humans, for instance. One of their most haunting hunting strategies was persistent hunting. Unlike many predators that rely on sudden bursts of speed or ambush tactics, humans employed sheer endurance. We would relentlessly track and pursue prey over long distances, exploiting a combination of unique traits that set us apart. First, our bipedal posture—walking and running on two legs—is an evolutionary advantage that allows us to cover vast distances more efficiently than quadrupedal animals. Unlike many other species, humans can run long distances with remarkable energy efficiency.

Another crucial factor is our ability to sweat. Humans possess an exceptional number of sweat glands, enabling us to cool our bodies more effectively than most animals. While other creatures must stop to pant or seek shade to prevent overheating, humans can maintain activity under scorching conditions, giving us a significant edge in prolonged pursuits.

Then there's our adaptability when it comes to nutrition. Humans are omnivores, capable of extracting nutrients from a wide variety of food sources. If food is scarce, our bodies turn to stored fat as fuel, allowing us to continue functioning—and running—even in times of starvation. This relentless capacity to endure hunger and hardship speaks to a terrifying level of resilience. The psychological component of human persistence is equally unsettling. Ancient hunts often ended not with a dramatic final struggle but with the prey succumbing to exhaustion and despair. Unlike humans, many animals cannot sustain prolonged exertion. As they overheat and tire, their bodies betray them. They slow, stumble, and ultimately collapse. At this point, the prey may try to flee, but its legs fail, its energy spent. The human, calm and deliberate, approaches to deliver the final blow. The inevitability of this outcome—the sheer relentlessness of the human hunter—is chilling.

What's even more unsettling is that humans are not the only persistence hunters in the animal kingdom; some species, such as African wild dogs, employ similar tactics. These animals are exceptional endurance hunters, relying on teamwork and relentless stamina to chase down prey over long distances. African wild dogs hunt in packs of 2 to 20 individuals, with each member playing a crucial role in the pursuit. They work together seamlessly, using their exceptional stamina to run their prey into exhaustion. Unlike other carnivores that rely on bursts of speed to ambush their quarry, wild dogs maintain a steady pace, keeping up the chase for hours, ensuring their prey becomes too tired to escape. Their strategy isn't just about physical endurance; it's about cooperation. Each dog takes turns leading the chase, sharing the burden so that no individual becomes too fatigued. This coordinated effort is what allows them to hunt successfully in the harsh African wilderness.

However, what sets humans apart is our ability to elevate this trait of persistence hunting through our ingenuity, adaptability, and capacity for complex social organization. While animals like the African wild dog rely on instinct and physical prowess, humans have used their cognitive abilities to transform hunting into an art of strategy and collaboration. Early humans learned to operate in groups, recognizing that collective effort is far more efficient than individual action. It's not just about chasing down prey—humans figured out how to manipulate the environment and create traps, craft weapons, and use tools to make hunting more effective. The use of tools was a game-changer: spears, axes, and later bows and arrows, all amplified our ability to hunt with precision and effectiveness.

Humans also devised intricate strategies to amplify the success of their hunts. For example, some groups used the tactic of driving herds of animals into enclosed spaces like ravines or narrow gorges, where they could easily be overwhelmed or trapped. Others used fire to herd animals, driving them toward areas where they could be killed more easily. These strategies required not only physical effort but also careful planning and timing—something that was beyond the capability of any other species. The human ability to plan and coordinate these strategies has only grown over time. Our reliance on language, which allowed us to communicate and share knowledge, enhanced our ability to work in larger and more organized groups. By collaborating, humans could share resources, protect each other, and improve their hunting techniques, making them more efficient and effective. Over generations, this cooperation expanded from hunting to more complex forms of social organization, like building societies and cities, where shared goals and tasks could be accomplished on an even larger scale.

Unlike other animals that hunt primarily for survival, humans have expanded the concept of persistence hunting to encompass power, control, and manipulation. The same skills that allowed our ancestors to survive in the wild have been repurposed in modern times to secure resources, dominate rivals, and even wage wars. Our relentless pursuit of goals, combined with our ability to adapt, organize, and create technologies, has led to a level of influence and impact that no other species has ever achieved. This amplification of persistence hunting through ingenuity and cooperation is what makes humanity so distinct. While animals like African wild dogs demonstrate the power of teamwork and endurance, humans take these basic instincts to new heights. Our tools, strategies, and cooperative abilities have allowed us to not only survive but to reshape the very world around us. What was once a simple hunt for food has evolved into a complex, multifaceted drive for dominance, influence, and control—an unstoppable force that has altered the course of history and continues to shape our future.

However, our terror goes far beyond persistent hunting. Hunting, in its early form, was a critical survival skill, an essential part of life for early humans. It enabled us to evolve, grow, and adapt to our environments. But as humanity advanced, progressing far past the age of fire and stone, the nature of our pursuits shifted. We developed tools, built societies, and invented complex technologies, all of which amplified our capacity for both creation and destruction.

With these advancements, we also became painfully aware of the true atrocities that humans are capable of—atrocities often committed not by the forces of nature, but by our own hands. Throughout history, humans have inflicted suffering upon each other in ways more brutal and incomprehensible than any predator-prey dynamic. We have waged wars for power, domination, and resources, and created ideologies that justify oppression and violence. Our most horrific acts are often perpetrated against our fellow humans, driven by fear, hatred, and greed. From genocide to slavery, from torture to the systemic dehumanization of entire groups of people, the atrocities we have inflicted on one another speak to a dark and deeply disturbing facet of our nature.

This capacity for self-inflicted horror is not just the result of external threats or the needs of survival; it speaks to a deeper, more insidious aspect of human nature—the ability to turn our intelligence and determination toward destruction. It's as though, in our evolution, we discovered the power not just to manipulate the world around us, but to manipulate each other, using our intellect and will to control, oppress, and annihilate. Beneath the surface of civilization lies an undercurrent of violence, exploitation, and hidden motives. Power dynamics, whether political, social, or economic, often mask the true intent of those in control: to dominate, to conquer, to ensure their own survival at the expense of others. In the realm of politics, this dynamic becomes even more pronounced. Politicians, often seen as leaders, are like dogs with loosened leashes, given the illusion of freedom, yet at any moment, they can be reeled back in by the unseen forces controlling them. The delusion of power they carry is just that— an illusion. They believe they hold sway over the masses, but in reality, they are puppets, controlled by hidden strings pulled by those who operate from the shadows. The true power is not in their hands, but in the hands of those who know how to manipulate them, using their ambitions as tools for their own agendas. What starts as a desire for power often ends in subjugation, as politicians, driven by personal gain or ideology, find themselves ensnared in a web of influence far greater than their own.

The media, too, plays a pivotal role in this dynamic. News outlets, in their race to be first to break a story, often resort to the Kuleshov effect—manipulating images, sounds, and words to create an emotional response that shapes public perception. They feed us stories designed not to inform, but to influence, steering our thoughts and beliefs in ways that benefit those in control. This manipulation often comes at the cost of truth, as the rush to be the first to say something often trumps the responsibility to say what is accurate. The result is a constant stream of half-truths, exaggerations, and outright fabrications that serve to control the masses, distracting them from the real issues, and keeping them passive, disoriented, and divided. What's terrifying is that the system we've built—political, media, and social—works to maintain this cycle. The power players in these arenas have learned to use our emotions, our biases, and our desire for information against us. The more we become accustomed to consuming information in this way, the more susceptible we become to being controlled. It's a subtle form of brainwashing, where the lines between reality and fiction are blurred, and where the truth is just another weapon in the hands of those who seek to dominate us. In this landscape, the battle isn't just for resources or territory—it's for control over our very minds. And in this relentless pursuit of power and influence, humanity's darker side thrives, pulling the strings of our collective fate from the shadows.

The question remains: will humanity ever fully unite? And if we do, how terrifying could we be as a united force? Imagine the full might of human ingenuity and persistence channeled into a single purpose. Even in the hypothetical case of an alien invasion, humanity's potential for destruction would be unparalleled. Picture an alien species arriving on Earth, unprepared for an onslaught by hordes of small, seemingly fragile creatures who are, in reality, relentless and ingenious enough to dominate their planet. These creatures have manipulated metal and chemicals into weapons capable of obliterating entire regions in seconds. But it's not just our weaponry that makes us formidable. Our existence itself is a testament to endurance and determination. When humans set their sights on a goal, we do not stop until it is achieved. Our fighting capacities are both barbaric and astonishing. Humans can sustain extreme physical damage, losing significant amounts of blood or enduring internal injuries, and still persist. This resilience, combined with an almost unfathomable tenacity, might be inconceivable to an alien species. Ultimately, what makes humanity so terrifying is not just our physical endurance or technological advancements, but the precarious combination of brute strength, relentless willpower, and unparalleled creativity. We are precariously brutish and extraordinarily intelligent, a duality that has allowed us to thrive—and dominate— against all odds. This is the human paradox: a species capable of both profound creation and unthinkable destruction, bound by an unyielding drive to endure and conquer.

Unfortunately, as I've mentioned, humans have inflicted some of the most horrific tragedies upon one another throughout history. These atrocities serve as stark reminders of the immense capacity for cruelty that exists within us. Among the most devastating examples are massive war crimes, such as the Holocaust, where entire groups of people were subjected to systematic extermination driven by hatred and ideology. These atrocities, though on a vast scale, are not isolated incidents. There are countless other examples—smaller but equally devastating— that reveal the darker aspects of human nature, often obscured by time and the limits of history's gaze.

Today, we continue to witness the horrors of humanity's inhumanity, such as the ongoing genocide in Palestine. The violence and oppression faced by the Palestinian people, particularly in Gaza, has reached catastrophic proportions. Thousands of lives have been lost, families displaced, and entire communities destroyed. This modern-day tragedy echoes the worst of our past, where one group of people imposes cruelty and suffering on another with horrifying efficiency. What is happening in Palestine is not just a geopolitical conflict; it is a profound violation of basic human rights that has left a profound scar on the global consciousness. At times, the greatest threat to humanity has not been external forces like an asteroid or natural disasters, but humanity itself. Our capacity for cruelty and destruction towards one another is a constant reminder that, despite our intellect and creativity, we are capable of actions that push humanity to the brink. This relentless drive to harm or dominate others has been one of our species' most defining features, and it is something we must confront head-on if we hope to avoid repeating the darkest chapters of history.

Consider the Black Death, a plague that casually wiped out roughly half of all humans on Earth in just five years during the medieval period. The scale of this event is almost unimaginable. Living during that time, surrounded by death, must have been a nightmare of unprecedented proportions. Earlier pandemics, such as the Plague of Justinian in 541 CE, killed approximately 30% of the population at that time. These events, along with numerous other pandemics, threatened humanity's very existence. Yet, time and again, our species has endured. If our ancestors hadn't valiantly pushed through these mass extinction events, we wouldn't be here today. This ability to recover, repopulate, and rebuild after devastating losses is what makes humanity so terrifying. We adapt and rebuild—over and over again. And yet, humanity's greatest threat continues to be itself. Our differences in ideals and beliefs have fueled some of the largest conflicts in history. These conflicts have driven us to create machines of destruction that have caused casualties on scales that defy humane comprehension. For instance, the concept of "Rods from God"—massive tungsten rods dropped from orbit with the destructive force of nuclear bombs—demonstrates our penchant for innovation in devastation. The concept wasn't abandoned because it was inhumane but because it was impractical and expensive. This relentless drive to protect ourselves from—and destroy—each other is a testament to both our ingenuity and our terrifying potential.

What's even more astonishing is the speed at which humans have progressed. Aliens—or any hypothetical observers—would likely be astounded by the pace of our development. Just 200 years ago, humans didn't have railroads. 125 years ago, airplanes didn't exist. 75 years ago, spaceflight was a mere dream. 35 years ago, the internet hadn't yet transformed our world. In a remarkably short span of time, we've not only inherited the Earth but are now setting our sights on the stars and whatever lies beyond. Yet, what's even more astonishing is how rapidly we've moved from simple tools to the most destructive technologies in existence. It took far more years for humanity to evolve from wooden spears to iron swords than it did to create weapons of mass destruction. The time it took us to go from crafting basic weapons for survival to developing nuclear bombs and technologies that can obliterate entire cities is staggeringly short in comparison. In just a few generations, we've gone from mastering fire to wielding the ability to reshape the planet itself. This acceleration of technological and destructive power is a profound reflection of our complex nature—where creativity and devastation are often two sides of the same coin.

If anything tries to stand in our way, history suggests we will annihilate it. Humanity's technological growth is not just impressive; it's accelerating.

Artificial intelligence is advancing at exponential rates, reshaping industries and societies at an unprecedented pace. Spaceflight is resuming with renewed vigor, and the prospect of exploring other worlds is within our grasp. Medical technology has extended our lifespans by nearly 50 years compared to ancient times, and our scientific breakthroughs continue to push the boundaries of what's possible. Our growth, in every sense, is nothing short of extraordinary. Yet, there's an unsettling aspect to this progress. Now, we are in such a hurry to replace all the work humans have done throughout history, sometimes even creating fake documentation or pretending that past achievements didn't happen. The thing about art, for instance, is that it's difficult even when you have all the right tools in front of you. But instead of fostering genuine creativity, we now seek to diminish our intelligence, dulling it to a point of no return. The drive to replace true human effort with artificial solutions—whether in the form of generated content, automated systems, or superficial imitations—reflects a troubling trend. We seem eager to erase the depth and complexity of human creation, in favor of efficiency and convenience. This relentless drive, adaptability, and ingenuity make humanity both a remarkable force and a terrifying one. We have the potential to conquer, innovate, and create, but also to destroy, undermine, and erase. It's this duality that makes us not just a species capable of extraordinary feats, but one that may ultimately be our own undoing.

And yet, humanity isn't just about destruction or endurance; it's also about preparation and ingenuity in the face of existential threats. Consider what happens when a genuine asteroid does threaten Earth. Astonishingly, we have a plan for that too. In 2022, NASA achieved what might be one of the most remarkable feats in recent history with the DART mission—humanity's first planetary defense test. NASA deliberately slammed a spacecraft into an asteroid to alter its trajectory, a groundbreaking experiment in safeguarding our planet. The asteroid, Dimorphos, was approximately 6.8 million miles away from Earth at the time. The spacecraft collided with it at an incredible 13,000 miles per hour, creating a crater about 33 feet across. The impact successfully shortened the asteroid's orbital period by 32 minutes. Think about that: humans managed to send a projectile across the vast emptiness of space and alter the trajectory of an asteroid in orbit. This is a level of precision and technological mastery that borders on the unbelievable. Space, once an insurmountable boundary, is gradually becoming another frontier for human exploration. The DART mission represents more than just a test of planetary defense; it's a symbol of humanity's growing ability to confront and overcome even the most distant threats. Slowly but surely, humans are chipping away at the glass ceiling of space travel. One day, we might shatter that ceiling altogether, reaching other planets. When that day comes, humanity's relentless growth and ingenuity will ensure that there's no turning back.

But I've been holding back on discussing one specific trait—one that truly cements humanity as the most terrifying force in existence: our boundless curiosity. This singular drive to explore, conquer, and understand has propelled humanity forward in unimaginable ways. It's a double-edged sword—both our greatest strength and the source of our most unsettling potential. Our curiosity compels us to climb mountains, even at the cost of lives, simply because they are there. It drives us to venture into space because the vastness of Earth feels limiting, and we yearn for more. It pushes us to uncover every hidden corner of our planet, not out of necessity but because we cannot stand the idea of leaving anything unexplored.

If I were an alien observing humans, I would be terrified. Our curiosity is relentless. We would likely stumble upon alien life by accident, find it fascinating, and subject it to rigorous investigation—not out of malice, but because we simply must understand. Humans are capsules of creativity, spirit, and courage. We leave our mark on every possible surface for those who come after us, driven by an innate desire to say, "We were here." In the grand tapestry of human existence, a paradox emerges: our capacity for greatness is matched only by our propensity for destruction. Just as termites infiltrate a structure, weakening its foundation until it collapses, our darker impulses can erode the very civilization we strive to build. Like termites, our actions often seem small and insignificant at first, yet they compound over time, creating cracks in the very systems meant to sustain us. This relentless infiltration by self-interest and unchecked ambition gnaws away at the stability of our societies, threatening to undermine even our most monumental achievements. Yet, within this capacity for destruction lies an equally overwhelming drive for creation and exploration. Humans are filled with both good and evil, forever caught in the struggle to choose between them. The bricks of civilization are infiltrated by our motives, and with each opportunity we create, we also lay the groundwork for new problems. This duality—of being both creators and destroyers—is what makes humanity so complex, so remarkable, and so terrifying.

This insatiable need to explore and conquer is ingrained in our DNA. Until every urge is exhausted, until we have fully mapped, conquered, and understood every frontier, we will not stop. And whatever stands in our way—be it a mountain, an ocean, or a cosmic barrier—will either step aside or be annihilated. All of this we do under the shadow of an existential question: why? Why are we here, conscious and aware, on a rock hurtling through the void of space? In many ways, humanity is a paradox. We are terrifyingly persistent and absurdly fragile. We are cursed with self-awareness, forced to confront the vast unknown of the universe every day. And yet, despite the overwhelming odds and the absurdity of our existence, we continue to strive. We persevere in the face of catastrophe, the unknown, and the seemingly insurmountable.

Oh, universe, tremble. For Earth has birthed an unforgiving force, and it looks upon you with relentless curiosity and desire. We are matter that decided to wake up, to reflect, and to create. We are significant, beautiful, and terrifying. Whatever stands in our path, we will push through, leaving an indelible mark on history and the cosmos alike. As a species, we will forge new paths, write new stories, and etch the name Homo sapiens deep into the fabric of existence. Humanity is terrifying, not because of what we are, but because of what we are capable of becoming.

Chapter 3

The Money Testament

"Money, that wretched idol, promises freedom but delivers only bondage. It is not difficult to accumulate wealth, for it flows easily to those who crave it, who bend the world to their desires. But to remain unchanged by it—this is the true struggle, the silent torment of the soul. In the pursuit of riches, one may lose everything that truly matters and yet never know it. For what is wealth, if not a veil over the heart, hiding the emptiness that grows with every possession? The true question is not how to stay rich, but how to keep one's soul from being consumed by the very thing that promises salvation."

Throughout history, men have created countless tools to shape their world—fire, the wheel, the plow—yet one invention stands above them all, not as a tool in the hand, but as an invisible yet omnipotent force: *money*. You may ask, "What is mankind's greatest invention?" Certainly, there are many answers: fire, that which tamed the night and warmed the body; the wheel, which turned the face of commerce and movement; or the plow, which made the soil bow to human will. But none of these are as insidious as money—this abstract *idea* that shapes us in ways we scarcely understand. Unlike fire or the wheel, money is not a tangible object; it does not burn or turn, it does not toil in the fields. No, money is the *idea* of value itself, and it binds us with invisible chains. It is the *will to power* of the herd, the means by which society's desires are mediated, controlled, and exploited. Money is the phantasm that drapes itself over the visible world and claims dominion over it. And yet, it is not real—this "value" is not something innate, but something we, the masses, have agreed upon. Money is the ultimate illusion. Unlike fire or the wheel, whose purpose is clear, money serves no one's true will but rather the will of the *lowest common denominator*—the crowd, the herd, the collective. It is not the thing itself that drives us, but the *desire* for it. The illusion of value is what keeps us chained to it. But what is this desire? It is nothing more than the desire for recognition, for the affirmation of one's worth in a world that seeks only utility. We chase money not for what it is, but for what it *represents*: power, status, control. This is the subtle trickery of money—it becomes the means of mediating the will to power of the individual in the context of the herd. And because it is accepted by the masses, it has the power to bind the individual to a system not of his own making, but of the society's creation. Consider this: you value money because you value the illusion it creates. This system, this belief in its importance, has replaced other more immediate, visceral truths of human life. It is a reflection of the sickness of society—the decay of spirit where value is no longer created by the individual's *will to power*, but by an external, abstract force that keeps all tied to the same wheel. In the end, this makes money not an invention of civilization, but a *product* of civilization's sickness. It is the product of a world that no longer values the strength of the individual, but instead seeks comfort in mediocrity. The masses, seduced by the glitter of money, forget that true power lies not in possession of wealth but in *transcending* the need for it. Those who *are* truly free do not seek to exchange their spirit for gold, but rather use their power to transcend the very idea of value that binds them to the herd.

However, the fact that money is an illusion does not undermine its importance. Before money existed, we had to rely on the barter system: people exchanging goods and services directly. But this system had its flaws. I remember an interesting experience I had in school that made me think about money differently. It was a Friday, and our English teacher had written the topic "Money: Pros and Cons" on the board, as was customary. That day, he picked one of our classmates, a student who wasn't one of the top performers, to give a lecture on the subject. He started with a well-known quote circulating on social media:
"With money, you can buy a house, but not a home. With money, you can buy a clock, but not time..."
He then began to contradict these lines by offering his own perspective:
"With money, you can hire someone to do your job and save time. With money, you can buy a house and create a home for your family..."
At this point, my friend, who was at the top of the class, began to argue. He disagreed with the speaker's

words, and while we all knew his point, the words weren't coming out clearly. The lecturer and a few of his friends, sensing the tension, jokingly said, "Well, toppers, give us your money then. You clearly don't place much value on it." We were all silent for a moment. Why would we give up the money we had earned as a cash prize for our high academic achievements the previous year?

Then, our teacher, who had been listening, shared a story of his own. He recalled a similar Friday when he had attended a lecture by a scholar on the very same topic. During the talk, someone from the audience tried to give the scholar some money. The scholar, however, had refused. But as the scholar was leaving, he felt something unusual in his shoes. To his surprise, it was the exact same amount of money that had been offered to him earlier. He picked it up and said to those around him, "This is the value of money: flat on the ground, but not denied of its value."

Our teacher smiled and continued, "You cannot deny money's necessity, just as you cannot deny the three basic needs of life—food, water, and shelter. Even if you are fortunate enough to have all these, you will still find yourself wanting something else to buy."

That conversation made me realize how, despite all our modern conveniences, we still struggle with the same fundamental issue that people faced long ago: the problem of exchanging value. In our case, we might not be directly bartering for goods like people did thousands of years ago, but in essence, we still rely on something to measure the value of the things we want and need.

For example, if I wanted vegetables for dinner but only raised cattle, I would have to trade an entire animal for a bag of vegetables. Similarly, if I made tents but needed shoes, I'd have to trade an entire tent for a pair of shoes.

Immediately, you can see the problems with this system: asymmetry. As a tentmaker, I might feel cheated if I had to trade a whole living space for something as simple as shoes. Without a standardized medium of exchange, it was difficult to find a fair trade between two people. Even more problematic was the "double coincidence of wants": you had to wait for someone who not only wanted what you had, but also had what you wanted in return. This was both inefficient and limiting.

Money, however, addresses these issues. It's not just a medium of exchange; it's also a store of value. Before money, some people couldn't store their wealth at all. Consider the farmer who grows tomatoes and the man who makes tents. The tentmaker can create real estate—something that can be traded year-round. But the farmer is limited by the seasons, and his tomatoes are perishable. So even if both individuals worked as hard, the farmer had no way to retain his wealth beyond harvest time.

This reminds me of a conversation I once had with my stepbrother Roman. One afternoon, as we sat at the dining table after lunch, I asked him if he had told our father about his decision to leave his studies and pursue business. He nodded, explaining how our father had set up a marble business for him with his paternal uncle, where they shared equal ownership.

His uncle was supposed to mentor him, but things didn't go as planned. Roman shared how his uncle betrayed him, forcing him to walk away from the partnership. At that moment, Roman had only $2.50 in his pocket. Yet, he wasn't afraid to leave. "The person I became during those years and the value I produced made me a name in the market," he said confidently. Using his skills and reputation, Roman started his own marble industry, which soared to success. Meanwhile, his uncle's business declined over time. Roman often spoke about the unique value of his work. "The type of marble I produce is only for the rich," he once told me. And he wasn't exaggerating. On numerous occasions, I saw wealthy and influential clients visiting him at home, seeking his expertise. His journey illustrated how money not only measures value but also serves as a tool for resilience and reinvention.

The issue gets more complex when certain goods aren't widely desired. Today, business advice often encourages people to find a niche—an audience small enough to support their product.

However, in a world where everyone is chasing success, the rise of self-proclaimed "gurus" complicates the understanding of wealth creation. Today, on the internet, everyone seems to be a guru promising to show you how to become a millionaire. These so-called experts often rent mansions and luxury cars to emotionally hook their audience, turning them into golden-egg-laying geese. Their strategy revolves around creating communities that ultimately serve to enrich the guru themselves. By buying their courses, people believe they're unlocking secrets to wealth, but in reality, they're often funding the guru's rented lifestyle.

These courses sell the dream of fast riches, prescribing routines and habits that supposedly guarantee success. If they pour into your cup, who is going to pour in their cup? Yet, the truth is that everyone's mind operates on different frequencies, and no one-size-fits-all formula exists for success. Instead of guiding people toward discovering their unique talents, many of these gurus exploit their followers' aspirations. Psychologist Carol Dweck's concept of a "fixed" versus "growth" mindset can help explain why this approach is problematic. Dweck's research shows that people with a "growth mindset" (the belief that abilities and intelligence can be developed) tend to embrace challenges and setbacks as opportunities for growth. In contrast, those with a "fixed mindset" (the belief that intelligence and abilities are static) may struggle to apply generic strategies or abandon them entirely when they don't work immediately. The reality is that everyone's mind, life circumstances, and opportunities are different, making a cookie-cutter approach to success ineffective for most. Moreover, many of these courses are vague on practical, actionable advice. A 2019 study by the *Consumer Financial Protection Bureau* revealed that a staggering number of self-help financial gurus provide content that lacks substance or proven methodologies, often relying on motivational speeches and generalized advice to keep viewers hooked. In some cases, the content may even be recycled or plagiarized from other sources. The focus is rarely on real education or empowerment, but rather on getting people to buy into the cycle of constantly purchasing new courses and "upgrades" as part of their journey to success.

They rarely admit that some "successful" students are earning money not from the course's teachings but through affiliate marketing schemes that funnel more people toward the guru.

I fell into the trap myself once. Like so many others, I was seduced by the promises of quick success, and I dismissed the slower, more traditional methods as outdated and inefficient. I remember scoffing at Warren Buffett's famous quote: *"Fast success builds ego, slow success builds character."* At the time, I thought he didn't understand the new, modern ways of making money—the ones that promised instant wealth with minimal effort. I was convinced that following the conventional, step-by-step path of hard work and persistence was a fool's game. I believed the key to financial freedom lay in seizing every opportunity, capitalizing on trends, and exploiting shortcuts to wealth.

But when I started my own business, reality hit me like a ton of bricks. The promises I had bought into, the flashy success stories and get-rich-quick schemes, all fell apart the moment I had to put them into practice. I failed miserably. I rushed headlong into the business world, thinking that the more sales I made, the faster the money would come. I wanted to scale quickly, focus on high-volume sales, and follow any tactic that seemed to promise instant profits. But I approached business with the wrong mindset—more focused on *how much* I could make than on *how much value* I was providing in return. That failure was a bitter pill to swallow, but it taught me an invaluable lesson. The truth about business isn't about how many sales you can rack up or how fast you can grow. It's about creating real value—value that goes beyond mere transactions and reaches into building trust, loyalty, and respect with your customers. I came to realize that business is not just about *selling* something; it's about providing a solution, solving a problem, or enriching someone's life in a meaningful way. And that requires honesty, integrity, and a deep respect for the people you serve. Many of us enter the business world with one goal in mind: to make money. But too often, we neglect to consider the deeper, core values that underpin long-term success. Quick sales might bring in immediate cash, but they won't build lasting relationships or sustainable growth. True success lies in respecting the money that customers trust you with, and ensuring that you provide value that matches or exceeds their expectations. It's not enough to just deliver a product or service—you have to build a reputation for reliability, quality, and consistency. You have to care about the experience your customers have with your brand. Building a sustainable business, one that stands the test of time, requires patience and dedication. It's about focusing on quality over quantity, relationships over transactions. The quick path to riches may seem alluring, but it is a mirage. It's the slow and steady work, the constant refinement, the perseverance through challenges, that build a foundation strong enough to weather any storm. In the end, it's not just about the profits you make—it's about the character you build along the way. And that character, forged through hard work and a commitment to doing things the right way, will be far more valuable than any quick win. True wealth, I've learned, isn't measured in dollars and cents; it's measured in the impact you have on others, the trust you cultivate, and the integrity you uphold in every deal, every transaction, every relationship. When you focus on providing real value, not just chasing profits, you lay the groundwork for something much more enduring: a legacy of respect, credibility, and lasting success. So while shortcuts might promise fast results, it's the long road—the one that teaches you resilience, patience, and honesty—that leads to true wealth, both financial and personal.

In the world before money, such a strategy would have left you with nothing to trade. Only those who owned universally desired goods—things like salt, weapons, or animal skins—could trade successfully. And because everyone wanted these items, people would stockpile them even if they didn't need them right away, setting the stage for commodity money. This was a way of exchanging goods and services for something that could be used later. Over time, commodities like shells, weapons, and even salt became representations of value.

The development of money marks a crucial turning point in human history. But what makes money so powerful, and why does its value seem to exist only because we believe in it?

The next leap was to create something easier to carry: metal coins. In 770 BC, China introduced the first metal coins. They were cast from bronze, a scarce material at the time, and were circular so they could be easily handled. This marked the first time money had intrinsic value based on the material it was made from—if you held a coin with one gram of gold, its worth was exactly that: one gram of gold.

But kings and rulers soon realized the power of money. They found that the more precious metals they controlled, the more power they could wield. By 600 BC, King Alyattes of Lydia (modern-day Turkey) minted the first official coins, using a mix of silver and gold. These coins were stamped with images to represent their value. But as rulers began to crave more money, they started reducing the precious metal content, diluting the value of the coins. Thus, the illusion of money was born: the value of the coin no longer depended on the metal it was made of, but on what people believed it was worth.

As time passed and international trade grew, the weight of metal coins became impractical. Kings started issuing IOU certificates—essentially paper promises to pay in metal coins. These certificates could be exchanged for coins, but over time, the value of the paper itself became detached from its metallic backing. By the time we reached the modern era, paper money had become the norm, and its value was determined solely by trust in the government that issued it.

Enter flat currency—a term that refers to money that has no intrinsic value but is decreed as legal tender by the government. This flat system means that money's worth is based entirely on people's faith in it. For instance, the 10,000 Singapore dollar note, which is no longer in circulation but still holds legal value, is worth around 7,345 US dollars today. Yet, it costs less than 20 cents to produce. The illusion is clear: the value of the paper money isn't tied to anything physical; it's determined by society's collective belief in it.

Flat currency is a delicate balance. For it to maintain value, it needs to be scarce. If too much is printed, the value of each individual unit decreases, leading to inflation. This is what happens when governments print money without a corresponding increase in the production of goods and services. In 2020, for example, the United States government printed more money than ever before to deal with the economic fallout of the COVID-19 pandemic. As a result, inflation surged, and the value of the dollar decreased. But here's where things get tricky: inflation is a natural consequence of printing more money. The more money in circulation, the less each dollar is worth. For example, in the wake of the pandemic, the U.S. printed an enormous amount of money, and as a result, the value of goods and services began to rise. A good illustration of this is the price of lumber, which tripled over the course of a year. Even everyday products, like a meal at your favorite restaurant, became more expensive. The result is that while people may have more money in their bank accounts, their purchasing power is eroded by inflation.

The government's ability to print money essentially creates a hidden tax on the public, which is why many economists and ordinary people alike worry about the future of flat currencies. And it's a vicious cycle. When governments spend more than they collect in taxes, they issue bonds or take loans. But eventually, those debts must be paid back, and the government often does so by printing more money. This further devalues the currency.

Take, for example, the U.S. government, which has been deeply in debt for years. In 2020, the U.S. debt was already over $29 trillion. But rather than pay down this debt, the Federal Reserve started buying back bonds, essentially printing more money to do so. While this might provide short-term economic relief, it also increases the amount of money in circulation and accelerates inflation.

But this isn't just about government debt; it's a wider issue that affects everyone. As more money is printed, the purchasing power of every dollar in your pocket decreases. As the dollar's value erodes, the price of assets like real estate and stocks may rise, making it appear that the economy is doing well. But in reality, it's a mirage—it's all denominated in a currency that's steadily losing value.

For example, if you measured the performance of the stock market, such as the Dow Jones, in terms of gold instead of dollars, you'd see that it's basically where it was in 1997. This shows the illusion of wealth. Stocks go up in value, but only because the value of the currency itself is shrinking.

So, what does all this mean for the future? Will the value of money continue to decrease indefinitely? Will the gap between the rich and poor keep growing wider? Or will we find a way to fix this problem that has plagued mankind for centuries? The answers to these questions are uncertain and will unfold over time, as we continue to navigate the complexities of a rapidly changing global economy. As the world becomes more interconnected and technological advancements reshape industries, the value of money and wealth distribution will undoubtedly be influenced by new factors. Yet, one thing is certain: understanding that money is merely an illusion—something that only has value because society collectively agrees on its worth—will guide us toward financial freedom. Money, in essence, is a construct—created by governments and financial systems to facilitate trade, measure value, and organize the economy. However, it is not an absolute or unchanging entity. Just as the value of money has been diluted throughout history through inflation, devaluation, and shifting global standards, so too will its meaning evolve in the future. This realization encourages a shift in how we view wealth. Rather than focusing on money as the end goal, we must understand it as a tool—a means to an end, rather than an end in itself.

In the modern world, it's easy to get caught up in the illusion that money equals success. Society often measures success by how much money one accumulates, yet true wealth is not necessarily monetary. True wealth lies in acquiring assets that transcend currency, such as skills, knowledge, relationships, and the ability to produce value. These are the things that will remain valuable, regardless of how the monetary system shifts. It's all a game—a game where avoiding total loss is the best anyone can hope for. But unlike a game of chance, the game of financial freedom requires strategy, awareness, and the willingness to think beyond short-term gains.

The key, therefore, is not to store wealth in currency alone, but to acquire assets that can outpace inflation and retain value over time. Physical assets like real estate, stocks, or precious metals—along with intangible assets like intellectual property, personal skills, and networks—are the true pillars of wealth. If you focus solely on accumulating money, you may find yourself left behind when inflation eats away at its purchasing power. But if you focus on building a portfolio of valuable, enduring assets, you equip yourself to weather any storm the financial world might throw your way. If you don't adopt this mindset, the game will play you. It's easy to fall into the trap of chasing after the next financial trend or investment fad, especially when the media and "gurus" offer alluring promises of instant wealth. But these shortcuts are rarely sustainable. Real, lasting financial freedom comes not from gambling with money but from strategic planning, long-term thinking, and continuously increasing the value you offer to the world. By focusing on acquiring assets that truly matter, you take control of the game, ensuring that your wealth is not subject to the whims of inflation, economic cycles, or financial speculation.

Chapter 4

The Curiosity Thieves

"In the modern age, there exists a tendency to reduce life to a spectacle—its most intimate moments dissected and offered as a form of entertainment, fragmented and shallow. This trend not only affects those who produce such content, presenting carefully curated pieces of their existence, but also those who consume it, drawn to the illusion of connection. Both groups, in their own ways, become ensnared in a cycle: one of perpetual creation for external validation, and the other of passive consumption, mistaking glimpses of another's life for something meaningful. In this exchange, the raw, unfiltered chaos of existence remains untouched, and a hollow form of connection takes its place, perpetuated by a fleeting sense of intimacy that ultimately holds no true substance."

In the 1980s and 1990s, advocates of free speech across the globe often argued that the media landscape was highly centralized and controlled. At the time, state-run television dominated most countries, with little to no alternative media outlets. Social media, as we know it today, didn't exist, so there were limited options for people to consume information or entertainment. The primary criticism was that these state-controlled media channels dictated what people could watch and, more importantly, what they couldn't—creating a kind of intellectual and cultural censorship. The argument was that citizens had very few choices in terms of what they could access and, more troublingly, the state didn't seem interested in allowing people to view content that could be enriching or empowering. Then came the internet. With its rise, many believed a new era of freedom was upon us. People could access any kind of content, watch any film, read any book, and explore countless documentaries or TV shows. The idea was that this vast repository of information would bring about a great intellectual awakening. People would become better informed, and the ability to deceive or manipulate them would be greatly diminished. There was even hope that traditional institutions like universities might lose their relevance, as self-education through the internet would empower individuals to teach themselves anything they wanted. The digital age, many hoped, would be a revolution of the mind.

However, the reality has turned out to be quite different. Modern society is grappling with a profound cultural crisis. Despite the vast ocean of information available to us, we have created a society that is increasingly driven by entertainment and superficial content. While we now have access to an endless array of videos, blogs, memes, and viral moments, much of this content is trivial, shallow, and devoid of substance. It has become entertainment for entertainment's sake, consumed mindlessly, often without any real message or deeper value. Rather than sparking intellectual growth or challenging societal norms, much of what we consume simply reinforces the status quo. This brings us to a significant issue— what we can call the "cancer" of modern digital culture: daily blogging. In an age where everyone can have a platform, there has been an explosion of content, much of it meaningless or trivial. Daily blogs and videos often focus on personal anecdotes, consumer products, or fleeting trends, devoid of any significant commentary or reflection. For example, consider the millions of people watching someone unbox a new iPhone and perform a dance or engage in some other banal activity. We watch these rituals, not for any intellectual enrichment, but out of sheer boredom or habit, feeding into an endless cycle of mindless consumption.

Simon Sinek highlighted this issue in a conversation with Steven Bartlett, reflecting on how vulnerability has been misconstrued in the digital age. He observed:

"I think we live in a world where we have confused vulnerability with broadcasting our feelings, right? And going on a podcast or worse, sitting in your bedroom with your phone on self-view and broadcasting your breakup or your anger or whatever it is on TikTok or whatever your medium of choice is, you know, is not vulnerability, even if you're crying. Have that exact same conversation with those exact same words with somebody you love and see how difficult that is. That's vulnerability. And I just, the idea of broadcasting everything, I think it's, you know,

putting pictures of me as a baby and my dad holding me and happy Father's Day, dad, I love you. My dad's not on freaking Instagram. Why don't I just call my dad and say happy Father's Day, I love you, as opposed to, like, I think it's hilarious. Our need to broadcast everything. And we think that's vulnerability, and it's not. It's broadcasting our emotions, which are different. So I think, you know, those conversations that you're struggling to have and, like, the ones that I won't share, it's not that I won't share them with anybody. It's that I won't share them with you. Because I like you, but you're not my soulmate. You're not the person that I confide in. I will absolutely share those deep, those things that I'm struggling with. But I'll share with somebody who can hold space for me. With love, not with the desire to make."

This performative sharing culture exemplifies the trivialization of human connection. As Sinek points out, the essence of vulnerability lies in intimate, genuine exchanges—not in curated digital displays for an anonymous audience.

We turn on our screens, mindlessly scroll, and consume whatever comes our way, then turn off our devices and go to sleep, as though nothing of substance has occurred. The issue is not the mere presence of entertainment; it's the overwhelming dominance of trivial entertainment in our lives. When we spend countless hours watching videos with no real educational or cultural value, we forfeit the opportunity to engage in more meaningful activities— like critical thinking, self-improvement, or genuine learning. As a society, we are in danger of confusing distraction with fulfillment, and in doing so, we risk losing our ability to think deeply and meaningfully about the world around us.

In sum, while the internet promised a new age of information and freedom, it has also created a landscape where superficial content often dominates, leading to a culture of consumption that feeds on the trivial and the inconsequential. We must ask ourselves: in an era where we have access to all the information in the world, are we truly using it to grow and evolve, or are we simply numbing our minds with the distractions of the digital age? Freedom of speech, at its core, is the ability to say the truth without hesitation rather than indulging in the noise of saying anything that's useless. While the internet provides a platform for everyone, this privilege is often squandered on trivialities rather than being used to elevate conversations or speak truth to power.

Now, if we look at the kind of content that fills the digital space, it becomes even more apparent how shallow and trivial it has become. Take, for example, the trend of people filming every mundane detail of their lives—where their every action, no matter how insignificant, is broadcast for all to see. Imagine a person preparing to cook a chicken. This isn't just any chicken, of course. We are invited to know the backstory, the sacrifices, and perhaps the personal reflections of the person as they make this simple meal. It's as if we are expected to find meaning in the most trivial of acts, transforming the ordinary into a spectacle. I thought fiction was just confined to imagination, written in books and portrayed in movies, but we started living it. Just by setting up a camera before falsely waking up, we have blurred the lines between reality and performance. This theatrical approach to life transforms even the most authentic moments into scripted scenes, designed to entertain rather than reflect truth. Then, there's the explosion of videos focused on consumerism. One popular video, for instance, might be titled "A Dream Come True: Buying a Million-Dollar Watch." The title alone gives a sense of grandeur and ambition, suggesting that acquiring such an item is a monumental achievement. In reality, it's a consumerist spectacle—a reminder of what we "should" aspire to, creating a society where material wealth is equated with success and happiness. And what is most troubling? Rather than feeling ashamed or motivated by our own lack of such extravagant items, we are glued to the screen, watching this individual flaunt their purchase for the sheer purpose of entertaining us. It speaks volumes about how we've come to equate entertainment with consumption. But it doesn't stop there. The content keeps pushing boundaries of absurdity. Another viral video might show someone daring a friend to shave his head bald for some kind of thrill or challenge, and millions of viewers watch this absurd spectacle unfold. This, too, becomes a form of entertainment— petty, empty, and devoid of any larger message or purpose.

Then there are the videos that delve into people's personal lives, often exposing intimate moments and trivial conflicts for the sake of views. One video could show a wife catching her husband smoking and slapping him in anger. Another might follow a couple through the various stages of pregnancy—documenting the wife's vomiting, delivering the baby, and everything in between. This kind of content, which plays on personal drama and intimate details, becomes fodder for the public's endless craving for entertainment. It is these small, often meaningless moments that captivate millions, but in doing so, they reduce our understanding of life to mere spectacle. What we're witnessing here is not merely the consumption of entertainment, but the creation of a culture that thrives on the trivial and the inconsequential. Every act, every gesture, no matter how insignificant, is turned into a commodity for public consumption. The deeper questions—about who we are, what we stand for, and where we're headed—are drowned out by the ceaseless noise of daily blogging, vlogging, and sensationalized content. We've allowed ourselves to become passive consumers of this digital circus, with little thought about the impact it has on our values, our understanding of the world, and even our sense of self-worth. This is what makes the current state of society so troubling. We have become so addicted to these petty distractions that we forget to engage with the real world, to challenge our assumptions, or to seek out more meaningful experiences. Despite the vast potential that many individuals possess, the pervasive emptiness of modern society leaves them unable to offer anything meaningful. Everyone seems empty, with nothing substantial to contribute, even when they have what it takes. The abundance of tools, platforms, and opportunities is squandered on trivial pursuits rather than on creating something of real value.

The focus on celebrity culture, material wealth, and shallow drama has overtaken more substantial pursuits, leaving us with an entertainment-driven society that promotes mindless consumption over critical thinking and personal growth. In the process, we've lost sight of the bigger picture. Rather than using technology and media to expand our horizons, we've allowed it to narrow our perspectives and define our lives by the shallowest of metrics—likes, views, and consumer purchases. Art, once a profound medium for expression, reflection, and societal critique, has increasingly devolved into a spectacle that prioritizes attention over authenticity. It has become a mockery of its own essence, with creators often favoring trends, shock value, or commercial appeal over depth and genuine creativity. The drive for virality and public validation has stripped art of its purpose as a mirror to society, reducing it instead to a commodity meant to entertain or provoke momentary reactions. This degradation is evident in the flood of content that masquerades as art but lacks thoughtfulness or originality. In this hollow pursuit, art no longer serves to challenge perspectives, inspire introspection, or evoke timeless emotions—it has been diluted to fit into the fleeting attention spans of a distracted audience. The irony is profound: in an age of unlimited creative tools and platforms, the art world, instead of flourishing, finds itself pandering to superficiality, making a mockery of its own potential to elevate humanity. And the more we feed into this culture, the more it grows, perpetuating a cycle of emptiness that leaves us craving something more meaningful, but never quite finding it.

This is the biggest news of the day, and everyone is expected to cherish it and have fun with it, because nothing more important is happening right now. There's no history more significant, no philosophy more pressing, no science or society more relevant, no facts, no art, no culture—nothing compares to this. But if someone starts smoking and gets into a petty argument with their spouse, millions of people will stop what they're doing, gather around, and watch it unfold. This is modern society, and this is its informed audience.

When we talk about democracy, we often imagine a society where the public is well-informed, where everyone knows what is happening in the world and within their own communities. There have been many changes, and a kind of revolution has unfolded in this country. Today, even the most uninformed individuals are aware of who manipulates the political system. Yet, despite these shifts, you will still find certain mainstream portals and platforms where discussions seem so intellectually elevated, you might believe that everyone participating is a philosopher—Plato, Aristotle, and perhaps even others who are beyond our understanding.

The question then arises: Who are the people consuming this kind of content, day in and day out, never missing a moment? They are not some otherworldly beings or mysterious creatures who have descended from the sky. They are not people with horns growing from their heads, nor are they aliens in disguise, dressed in superhero costumes to signify their status. No, these are the people you see around you every day—people whose actions and behaviors you witness constantly. The ones who, if asked to sit quietly for just 15 minutes, would struggle to endure their own presence. They are people who cannot tolerate stillness, who need constant psychological stimulation. Their minds demand an endless flow of thrills, enjoyment, and excitement, all the time. The reason they crave this is simple: without it, they would be forced to confront themselves. They would have to face their own darkness, their own unresolved issues. And that is something they cannot bear. They lack the courage to stand in front of their inner turmoil. They are weak, unable to process their problems or even acknowledge them. For these individuals, the easiest option is to escape—by indulging in content that provides immediate gratification and distraction. It's a way to avoid confronting the deeper questions about their lives. They consume content in such a way that the reward comes not from reflection or growth, but from the consumption itself. It's about fleeting pleasure, not about bettering the self. And this is the culture we've built—a culture where the easiest path is the one that offers temporary relief from the discomfort of reality.

At the core, these are the people who, when faced with boredom, will try anything to escape it, without giving a second thought to the consequences of their actions. Yuval Noah Harari once said, "Society suffers from too much excitement; we need boredom." In other words, we've become so obsessed with the constant need for stimulation and thrill that we've lost touch with the value of quiet reflection and stillness. Harari argues that we need more "boring" politicians, more "boring" times—an invitation to embrace simplicity and calm. Modern society, however, has become a victim of this obsession with excitement. People feel compelled to seek out constant thrills, as though boredom is something to be feared. The need for excitement has become pervasive: it's not enough to go out and enjoy a meal; now, you have to document it on social media. If you take a drive, it's not just about the drive itself—it's about sharing 10 different stories on Instagram, telling the world where you went, what you saw, and every little detail along the way. Even something as simple as buying a packet of biscuits becomes an event to be shared.

And it doesn't stop there. These people want to know every trivial detail of your day—where you stood, when you hit the brakes while driving, what color suit you were wearing, and the name of the burger you ate. They're curious about how much the chocolate you bought cost, the brand of your shoes, the label on your t-shirt, and even the brand of the cap you're wearing. They want to know everything—where you're partying, where you're going, and what you're doing—because, for them, it fills the void left by their own lack of engagement with anything deeper or more meaningful. This kind of obsessive sharing and consumption of minute details isn't just about connecting; it's about filling an empty space with noise. These individuals are constantly looking for something to entertain them, to distract them from the silence and the introspection that might otherwise force them to confront their own inner world. The result is a society where real engagement with life—whether it's political, intellectual, or emotional—takes a backseat to the trivial and the performative. What we're left with is a culture driven by the need for constant novelty, where the smallest, most insignificant details are treated as newsworthy simply because they provide a brief moment of entertainment. It's an endless cycle of distraction, where the most important thing is not living meaningfully, but having something to post.

Imagine being born into this world, on this vast planet filled with millions of topics and experiences that could spark your curiosity and drive your mind. There are endless possibilities to explore, countless things that could ignite a sensation in your mind. Yet, amidst all of this, someone chooses to engage with the very topic I just mentioned. And they might think, "What have I lost? I was free anyway, so I invested my time into this." But here's the reality: *your time is wasted. Your attention is wasted.* What you've gained in exchange for your time and focus has added no value, only contributing to a sense of emptiness. If you believe this is merely an activity for fun, it will eventually lead to your downfall. Just wait and see. The first thing Yuval Noah Harari points out is that boredom is necessary. If someone cannot accept boredom, they will never be able to do meaningful work. Consider the analogy of physical exercise: when you climb a mountain or engage in strenuous physical activity, your body gets covered in sweat, injuries occur, and blood may be shed. Your muscles tear, and fatigue sets in. There's no immediate enjoyment in that process, but the growth lies in the challenge. Growth comes from pushing yourself beyond your comfort zone. Yet, the people who consume shallow, distracting content are often the same ones who shy away from any form of challenge, craving the easiest, most comfortable life possible. They watch others engage in effortless entertainment and, in turn, regress into that mindset. Another issue is that they are the ones who took consumer culture to its peak. These individuals will make countless videos about trivial things: buying a small item, changing their car, or documenting the most mundane events— like their car getting into an accident, being stolen, or being sold. And the cycle continues with every little event. Meanwhile, children and young viewers are swept up in this shallow spectacle, fixated on every detail. It's a culture of overconsumption, where even the smallest life updates are presented as a form of entertainment, further reinforcing a cycle of distraction.

I've repeatedly noticed something troubling: children in fifth and sixth grade come to school and tell their parents, *"He's my friend, and he has a Range Rover."* I've also seen this reflected in blogs and social media where influencers showcase their new cars, portraying a lifestyle that is anything but ordinary. The issue is that these kids are getting depressed after watching bloggers who seem to change cars every week. They see this as an ideal lifestyle, consuming every modern luxury—latest iPhones, expensive watches, Adidas sneakers—and traveling on six international tours a year. What's worse, these influencers don't appear to be doing any work. Meanwhile, we go to school, get scolded, endure insults, do hard work, and strive to build a career. On the other hand, these bloggers wake up in the morning, say "hello" to the camera, get millions of views, pocket the money, and carry on as if nothing else matters. The kids look at this and think, *"What is this life? I want this too."*

This comparison game is taking a heavy toll on young minds. Kids, who have nothing inherently bad in their lives, are falling into depression and even contemplating suicide. I've seen it firsthand. The unrealistic comparison to the *perfect* life showcased by these influencers is distorting their perception of reality. A study by the National Institute of Mental Health (NIMH) found a troubling connection between social media use and the rise in suicides among teenagers. The constant exposure to idealized lives online, particularly through influencers and bloggers, is linked to growing mental health issues in young people. The pressures of comparing themselves to the "perfect" lives portrayed online, filled with material success, glamorous travel, and flawless appearances, can lead to feelings of inadequacy, isolation, and hopelessness. For many teens, these comparisons can become overwhelming, with some even contemplating suicide. The study emphasizes how social comparison theory plays a critical role in this process, as adolescents measure their self-worth against the highly curated, idealized versions of others' lives. The more time spent on social media, the more these negative feelings intensify, further contributing to a decline in mental well-being.

They begin to think that this is what an ideal life looks like: constantly exciting, full of family dinners, friends, parties, and laughter. There seems to be no challenges, no struggles. But here's the truth: all of this is scripted. These influencers aren't showing their real struggles or depression on camera. They've created a facade of perfection to sell to you. Their lives, too, have ups and downs, but they'll never show you the darker sides. They're not foolish enough to display their personal conflicts or stress. When they trim hours of footage, what you see is a curated, perfect version of their life—a product that's been carefully edited for maximum appeal. And that's what they're selling: a product of perfection. These lifestyle bloggers and YouTubers are creating a culture of consumerism that convinces young people that the purpose of life is to acquire things—whether it's new cars, designer watches, diamonds, or frequent international travel. If you don't do these things, they subtly imply, maybe you don't even deserve to be alive. They send the message that if you haven't accomplished this *ideal* lifestyle, your life is meaningless. This is a dangerous mindset, one that can lead people to feel that without these material accomplishments, their life isn't worth living.

And the worst part? There is no educational value in any of this. It's just endless consumption and comparison, with no real content that adds value to your life.

I'm not saying that my critique is about bringing your family on camera or that you should feel ashamed of it. This isn't a right-wing critique of family vlogging. Instead, my criticism is directed at the lack of substance and the shared superficiality of bloggers who are selling an empty, manufactured version of life to people—and even to their children. What's troubling, however, is not that these bloggers are profiting from it. They're doing their job, and they're doing it well, so there's nothing wrong on their end. They're empowered by their work, and they're maximizing their journey in the way they see fit. But what's the cost of all this? The real issue is that your time is being wasted, and your children are growing up idealizing a false, perfect lifestyle that doesn't exist in reality. Day in and day out, they watch these bloggers buy new houses, showcase luxurious lifestyles, and document every moment—from family holidays to religious festivals—all for content. But what are you gaining from this? They're selling you the bare minimum, with little to no depth, and people are consuming it without question. If there's even one percent of real talent involved, let me ask: what are you truly learning from this? What valuable insights or skills are being shared? This isn't about innovation or creativity; it's about conformity. It's about doing what everyone else is doing because one person has become popular, and now everyone follows them mindlessly. People don't stop to ask what's being offered or whether it adds any value to their lives. It's all about trends. Just because something is trending doesn't mean it's worth consuming.

This brings me to an interesting point about modern language and how it's been affected by this culture of viral trends. Words like "viral" used to be associated with diseases like the flu or influenza. But today, "going viral" refers to something entirely different— an idea or piece of content spreading rapidly across the internet, often without any real substance. It's as if we've been conditioned to care more about the popularity of things than the value they provide. There's a powerful concept discussed in the book *The Denial of Death* by Ernest Becker, which I highly recommend reading. Becker's work touches on the non-conformist idea of discovering and expressing one's true talent and unique purpose. He asks, "What is your true gift, your authentic vocation? In what ways are you truly unique, and how can you dedicate your uniqueness to something greater than yourself?" This is the essence of personal growth and fulfillment—finding your own voice, not simply following the crowd because it's popular. But in the age of social media, that deeper exploration of authenticity has been replaced with mindless consumption of trends and empty content.

Let me ask you this: among all these people creating content, is there anyone who can truly become a thought leader? Now, you might say that entertainment exists for the sake of entertainment, but I find that argument rather shallow. Entertainment should not be limited to simply making people happy or causing them to laugh—it should come with purpose and meaning. We should strive to go beyond just pleasing ourselves; there should be depth in what we consume and create. But what we see today is just an exercise in conformity. If someone is gaining popularity by talking about cars, then others simply follow suit, thinking, "I want to do that too." This pattern of consumption is not only repetitive but also mind-numbing. I've heard people say in private conversations, "Did you see that blogger? She bought a new Range Rover, and a new house! Or that guy, he's making so much money, I don't know how he's doing it, but he's out there living his dream." Society will idealize these people, and they will become the cultural heroes of this generation. But what does that mean for us? It's the decline of meaningful content.

Research shows that the majority of those consuming this type of content are children and women, groups that are already so influenced by external expectations. They are being exposed to this shallow, materialistic content, which only further distorts their perception of self-worth before they even have a chance to discover who they really are. What we have here is an entertainment spectacle that replicates drama for drama's sake. People tune in to see the most trivial things—someone waking up pregnant, someone painting their car, a person getting a fancy new PPF coating on their car, or even a ridiculous challenge where someone jumps into water. There are even blogs made about these absurd, fabricated events, with nothing of real substance behind them. And yet, these become the "thought leaders" of modern times. In today's world, truth has become something that only exists if it is validated by the masses. If enough people agree that something is true, it gains traction and becomes "real" in the eyes of society. So, when 80 percent of the audience is watching this content and idolizing these influencers, what are we actually worshiping? Low-effort content. People wake up, say a few words, film themselves doing trivial things, upload it, and get millions of views. It's the perfect formula for shallow fame. Meanwhile, many of us are grappling with ideas and topics that have been on our minds for months. We want to refine our thoughts, create meaningful content, and contribute something of value—but it's challenging. We have ideas, but we lack the time or resources to properly express them. And here comes the contradiction: while some of us struggle to create well-thought-out content, others are pumping out low-effort blogs every day.

It's the same for political bloggers: they create content based on whatever drama is happening at the moment and sell it to the public. But, I ask you—where do they find the time to think deeply? Where's the substance? Did any of these blogs add real value? Did they improve lives even in the slightest? The answer, unfortunately, is no. It's a cycle of shallow, low-effort content that offers nothing but distraction. It doesn't challenge us, doesn't encourage personal growth, and doesn't provide any meaningful insight. It's just noise.

The second issue is that by consuming this constant stream of content, we lose touch with what true pleasure and true pain are. When you become addicted to dopamine, constantly seeking thrill, you can't sit still with a bit of discomfort or tension. The moment you feel even the slightest unease, you immediately try to escape it. Diogenes, the ancient Greek philosopher, believed that by intentionally seeking out and enduring pain and hardship, he was actually living the most pleasurable life possible. Why? Because when you become accustomed to hardship, the simplest of pleasures—like feeling the warmth of the sun on your skin—become profoundly joyful and gratifying. The problem with today's content-driven culture is that if we never experience the opposite of pleasure—pain, struggle, or discomfort—we can't fully appreciate or even recognize what genuine happiness feels like. When everything's made easy and constantly pleasurable, any fleeting moments of joy or fun feel shallow and short-lived. They might last only a few minutes, and then they're gone. The problem arises when we begin to crave more and more, chasing the next high, the next thrill, in an endless loop. Over time, this constant pursuit of immediate gratification drains us, both mentally and emotionally, and leaves us exhausted. In today's world, success is measured by how much attention you can grab. The more attention you get, the more successful you are. This has replaced the older, more thoughtful definitions of success. Think about it: back in the day, a circus performer would jump through hoops or perform a daring stunt to gather a crowd. Now, it's the more outrageous and cheap behavior that draws attention—acting in increasingly sensational ways to rack up views. The more bizarre or shocking you act, the more social currency you accumulate. People's children look up to these influencers and say, "I want to be like them." But where has the intellectual class gone, the class that should be idealized for its thoughtfulness and contributions to society? Where are the role models who promote critical thinking and wisdom? Modern society has become incredibly efficient, informed, and self-aware, but there is a deeper issue: we are increasingly prioritizing surface-level success and validation over genuine intellectual and emotional depth. The lifestyle of perfection being sold through these platforms is, in fact, a complete disaster. The irony is that these influencers are making millions from this hollow entertainment—and, truth be told, they should be. If people are willing to sell their souls to this empty spectacle, it's not their fault. They're simply capitalizing on an audience that has already set itself up for self-destruction.

Neil Postman, in his seminal book *Amusing Ourselves to Death*, argued that in modern America, people don't really talk to each other anymore—they entertain each other. This observation is more relevant now than ever. We've stopped engaging in meaningful discourse and have instead turned to mindless entertainment. In the process, we lose the ability to differentiate between what truly matters and what's simply a distraction. The result is a society filled with noise, but very little substance.

Try this in a gathering of friends: bring up a serious topic, something intellectual, and speak about it for two to four minutes. Watch what happens. Half of them will get up and walk away, the other half will probably mock you or belittle you. Why? Because the ability to sustain a serious, scholarly conversation has become obsolete. It's not engaging anymore, it's not appealing. What's appealing now? It's the instant gratification of shallow, mindless content. This shift in what captures attention has deep consequences, and if you think the millions of views these bloggers get are solely their fault, you're mistaken. The problem goes beyond them; it's a collective issue.

There's a book called *Art and the Creative Unconscious* by Eric Neumann, in which he writes something incredibly profound: "But let us be careful when we speak of our society. If this art is degenerate, then we too are degenerate, for innumerable individuals are suffering the same collapse of the cultural canon, the same alienation, the same loneliness—the rising blackness with its shadow and devouring dragon. The disintegration and dissonance of this art are our own; to understand them is to understand ourselves. The destruction of culture and art is not just the destruction of art, it is our destruction as well." This quote encapsulates the heart of the issue. We've created a generation of minds that consume content mindlessly, 24/7. We are addicted to the noise, to the drama, to the sensation. And then, these content creators are born, products of this culture. They didn't emerge from a vacuum; they are the result of our collective disenchantment with meaningful content, our disdain for history, and our disconnection from deeper truths. To protect our children from this, we need to recognize that it's not just about stopping them from watching a few videos—it's about protecting them from a mindset, from a culture that thrives on the surface and avoids anything deep.

Carl Jung once said, "Indeed, it is becoming ever more obvious that it is not famine, not earthquakes, not microbes, not cancer, but man himself who is man's greatest danger to man, for the simple reason that there is no adequate protection against psychic epidemics, which are infinitely more devastating than the worst of natural catastrophes." I believe we are witnessing the rise of mass psychosis, a collective psychological breakdown. People are losing touch with reality, and it's getting worse. You see it in the younger generation, particularly with today's children. They're constantly tethered to their screens, disconnected from the natural world, from real-life experiences, and it's slowly eating away at them.

We belong to a generation that just wanted to go outside and play, even if it meant getting scolded by our parents or punished for being outside too long. We were made to engage with the world around us— whether in the mountains, by the river, or simply observing the sky. The benefits were clear: we learned resilience, patience, and appreciation for the simplest pleasures in life. But today, the concept of engaging with nature, of simply sitting in silence or having meaningful debates, is foreign to many. For today's children, everything is "boring" or "pathetic," as they struggle to find entertainment in the world around them. They've been conditioned to think that only flashy, quick thrills matter. They are victims of a culture that thrives on ambiguous, transient moments, where the past, present, and future blur into a constant cycle of distraction. And what's the result? A lost future, a generation unable to face the challenges of life because they've been raised on easy distractions and a lack of mental toughness. If we want to save them, we need to help them build mental resilience. They must learn to accept that challenges, difficulties, and pain are part of life—and that without suffering, there is no true happiness. No one can experience lasting joy without first understanding hardship. Without struggle, there is no meaning to happiness, and without meaning, happiness is fleeting. This is the message we need to pass on: that true growth comes from enduring pain, from overcoming adversity, and from learning to find meaning in life's challenges. Only then can one truly appreciate the joys and pleasures that life offers.

Chapter 5

The Relativity

"Perspectives are the prison bars of the mind—each man locked within his own view, convinced it is the only one that matters. But what is truth, if not a myriad of perspectives, each one as fleeting and fractured as the light on the surface of a vast, endless sea? To transcend is not to see the world as it is, but to break free from the tyranny of a single vision, to embrace the chaos of all possible truths and dance with the infinite contradictions of existence."

The Theory of Relativity, formulated by Albert Einstein in the early 20th century, forever altered our understanding of time, space, and the fundamental laws of the universe. Through this theory, Einstein proposed that time and space are not fixed entities but rather are flexible, relative to the observer's speed and position. This groundbreaking idea shifted the very foundation of physics, opening up new possibilities for exploring the cosmos. However, it wasn't just within the confines of scientific research that relativity would begin to leave its mark. During my time in college, I met a person who profoundly expanded my understanding of the concept—Muhaimin. He wasn't a physicist, nor did he have a deep academic interest in the laws of physics, yet in our conversations, he revealed to me an entirely different dimension of relativity. Through him, I began to see how the principles of relativity extended far beyond equations and experiments, touching on our perceptions of time, relationships, and the very way we navigate life. Muhaimin's perspectives opened the door to a broader interpretation of relativity—one that reached into the complexities of human experiences. It was as though I had been handed a new lens to view not only the universe but also the nuances of everyday life. Through this encounter, I learned that the laws of relativity, in their most profound sense, are not limited to the realms of physics—they also govern our relationships, our memories, and our very existence in a constantly shifting world.

When my school years came to an end, I faced a significant decision: choosing a college. I opted for one close to home, not because it had the best reputation but because it was convenient. The college was near enough for me to pick up and drop off my sister, creating a sense of routine and familiarity that I appreciated. My belief was clear: *Success isn't determined by where you are, but by your willingness to change yourself.* While most of my schoolmates were already planning to get into the most prestigious colleges with high status, I made a conscious choice to attend Qurtuba College—a decision grounded in practicality rather than prestige.

It was during this time that I met Muhaimin. At first, I didn't think much of him—he was a backbencher, funny, and had a wholesome personality. What drew me to him initially was how strikingly similar he looked to my cousin. I never spoke to him directly at first, but eventually, he found his way toward me. Muhaimin was unlike anyone I had met before. He was a person who seemed to operate on a completely different wavelength, one that allowed him to adapt to the frequencies of those around him. To put it simply, in the presence of "dumb" people, he played along, but in the company of those who were intellectually sharp, he matched their energy with his own brilliance. What truly stood out to me, however, was Muhaimin's deep love for physics, especially his fascination with the concept of *relativity*. He was constantly talking about it, not in the narrow context of scientific theory, but in a way that applied to all aspects of life. "Here comes the relativity," he would often say, whenever someone made a statement or gave an opinion. He would casually add that *what worked for one person might not work for another*. To him, the idea of relativity wasn't confined to the abstract world of physics. He saw it as a fundamental principle that governed how people saw and experienced the world—each person's perspective shaped by their own unique background, circumstances, and mindset. For the first time, I met someone who wasn't confined to a single view of the world. Muhaimin understood that everyone perceives things differently—based on their own experiences and personal histories. He would often say that the same event could be interpreted in countless ways by different people. What I saw as success, for example, might look like failure to someone else, depending on their perspective. It was a radical shift in my thinking:

Muhaimin wasn't just talking about the theory of relativity as a scientific principle. He was applying it to the human experience, showing me how perception itself could be a relative experience, shaped by factors far beyond one's immediate control.

l. Cultural Relativity:

As I continued to reflect on the idea of relativity, I realized that the concept wasn't limited to personal experiences or the physical world alone. It began to expand in my mind, revealing the ways in which cultural contexts shape the values, norms, and moral frameworks we live by. This was a new layer of understanding: *Cultural relativity*—the recognition that moral and social norms are not universal truths but are influenced by the society and culture in which we are immersed.

What I began to understand is that each culture has its own set of beliefs about what is right, what is normal, and what is acceptable. For example, in some cultures, familial loyalty is a key virtue, and individuals are expected to prioritize family obligations above all else. In others, individual freedom and personal achievement are given higher value, often leading people to pursue their own goals—even at the expense of family or community expectations. These values, though seemingly different, are not wrong in their respective contexts; they are simply products of different cultural perspectives. The idea that these beliefs are relative, shaped by our cultural environments, began to resonate with me deeply. I began to see that what one person might view as a universal truth could, in fact, be a cultural construct, shaped by where they come from and the environment they grew up in. A simple act, like a handshake, could mean entirely different things depending on the culture you were part of. What is considered polite or respectful in one society could be seen as offensive or inappropriate in another. The realization that there is no single, universal way to define "right" or "wrong" was a profound shift in my thinking. In fact, it made me realize that our moral and social frameworks are just as relative as the very experiences we live through. At first, this idea was unsettling. It felt strange to think that there might not be one absolute standard by which to judge human behavior or values. But as I reflected more, I began to understand the richness of this concept. Just as in physics, where time and space bend depending on one's frame of reference, our values, beliefs, and norms shift according to the culture we belong to. This idea of cultural relativity helped me see the world not as a place of fixed, universal truths but as a complex, dynamic system, where each culture holds its own perspective, shaped by its unique history, environment, and experiences. Rather than seeing the differences between cultures as conflicts or barriers, I began to appreciate them as diverse ways of understanding the human experience. It became clear to me that there is no one-size-fits-all approach to life. Just as the laws of physics can vary depending on your perspective, so can our values and perceptions of the world. Embracing this view opened my mind to the idea that our differences are not something to judge or dismiss but to understand and celebrate. The concept of relativity—so deeply rooted in science—was beginning to shape the way I thought about not just the physical world, but the social and cultural world as well.

As we delve deeper into the idea of relativity, it's important to understand that it doesn't just apply to our personal experiences or the physical world—it also shapes how entire societies approach fundamental concepts like justice, happiness, and identity. These ideas, while central to human experience, are not universal. Rather, they are deeply influenced by the cultural context in which we live, and understanding this is key to appreciating how the world works in different places. Take, for example, the concept of *justice*. Different cultures define justice in vastly different ways. In some societies, justice is primarily about enforcing laws through punishment. In others, it might focus on reconciliation, rehabilitation, or restorative practices aimed at healing the community. What one society considers to be a fair punishment, another might see as excessive, while some may even question the idea of punishment altogether. This shows us that justice is not a one-size-fits-all concept; it's a value shaped by the needs, priorities, and history of a particular society. Similarly, the concept of *happiness* is far from universal. In individualistic societies, happiness is often tied to personal achievement and self-expression. The idea that "happiness is personal fulfillment" resonates deeply, where individuals pursue their goals and desires to feel content. In contrast, in more collectivist cultures, happiness may be seen as something that's tied to social harmony, familial well-being, and community success. In these societies, happiness isn't just about personal success; it's about how one's life contributes to the greater good. So, while happiness might mean pursuing individual dreams in one place, in another, it could mean nurturing relationships and maintaining the balance of the community. Now, think about *identity*. How do we define ourselves? The answer to that question isn't fixed, because how we see ourselves is influenced by the culture we belong to. In some societies, identity is deeply tied to family and social roles. A person's identity might be defined by their responsibilities to their family, their status within the community, or the legacy of their ancestors. On the other hand, in more individualistic societies, identity might be based on personal choice, self-expression, and independence. In these cultures, identity is something you create for yourself, often through your actions, career, and the relationships you choose to form. What makes someone *who they are* is shaped by the societal values they grow up with. What this all shows us is that concepts like justice, happiness, and identity are not fixed truths. They are relative to the culture we come from. Just like how the laws of physics change depending on your point of reference, the ways we understand justice, happiness, and identity shift based on our cultural surroundings. In some cases, what's considered "right" or "just" in one society might seem completely out of place in another. And this doesn't mean one is wrong and the other is right—it simply means that these values are shaped by different cultural contexts. By recognizing this, we can begin to appreciate the richness and diversity of human experience. Understanding cultural relativity teaches us that there is no one way to see the world, no single definition of what is "right" or "true." Instead, there are as many truths as there are cultures, and each is valuable in its own right. Embracing this perspective opens up a broader view of humanity— one that doesn't judge or compare but seeks to understand and appreciate the many different ways people interpret the world. This is where the importance of understanding and respecting cultural differences becomes paramount. When we approach others' values and practices with an open mind, we avoid the trap of imposing our own standards and instead, allow for a more meaningful exchange of ideas. It's easy to assume that our cultural norms are universal, but the truth is, they are deeply rooted in our upbringing and experiences. By understanding that others have grown up in environments with different influences, we can begin to see that their ways of thinking, acting, and perceiving the world are equally valid, even if they seem unfamiliar or contradictory to our own.

Respecting cultural differences isn't just about tolerance—it's about embracing diversity as a strength. It allows us to build bridges rather than walls, to foster connections instead of divisions. In every culture, there is wisdom and insight shaped by centuries of tradition and experience. When we take the time to listen and learn, we broaden our own perspective and enrich our understanding of what it means to be human. Moreover, understanding cultural differences can prevent misunderstandings and conflicts. When we recognize that certain behaviors or attitudes are not universally understood, we become more mindful of how we communicate and interact with others. This awareness leads to more harmonious relationships, whether in personal friendships, business collaborations, or international diplomacy. It helps us avoid the pitfalls of ethnocentrism, where we judge others based on the standards of our own culture, and instead adopt a more inclusive approach that values multiple viewpoints. In a globalized world, where interactions across cultures are inevitable, this understanding becomes even more essential. As we engage with people from diverse backgrounds, whether through travel, work, or online communities, our ability to navigate cultural differences with respect and humility determines the success of these interactions. The more we open ourselves to learning about other cultures, the more we discover the vast, complex tapestry of human experience that enriches our lives. Ultimately, embracing cultural differences challenges us to step outside of our comfort zones and expand our worldview. It teaches us that our way of thinking is just one of many, and that by appreciating the variety of perspectives around us, we grow as individuals and as a society. Understanding and respecting cultural differences isn't just a moral imperative—it's an opportunity to learn, to connect, and to build a more empathetic and cooperative world.

Exploring the concept of cultural relativity naturally leads to greater empathy and deeper connections with others. When we accept that each culture defines its own values, norms, and practices based on its unique history and context, we begin to move beyond judgment and toward understanding. This shift in perspective is crucial in fostering empathy—because instead of seeing others through the lens of our own cultural standards, we learn to approach them with an open mind, eager to learn from their experiences and viewpoints. Cultural relativity teaches us that what might seem unusual or even "wrong" to us is often perfectly logical and meaningful within another cultural context. For example, what is considered respectful or rude, how authority is viewed, or how time is valued can vary dramatically across cultures. When we recognize that these differences are not signs of moral failure or backwardness, but reflections of distinct cultural frameworks, we begin to let go of rigid judgments and replace them with curiosity and acceptance. This shift allows us to cultivate deeper connections with people from diverse backgrounds. Empathy thrives when we acknowledge that others' actions and beliefs are rooted in the realities they've experienced. It encourages us to ask questions, listen actively, and embrace the opportunity to learn. For instance, understanding that a person's actions are guided by the expectations of their family, community, or society, rather than imposing our own assumptions, fosters meaningful dialogue. We no longer view cultural differences as barriers to connection, but as windows to a greater understanding of each other's humanity. Furthermore, empathy grows when we stop assuming that our own way of thinking is the "right" way. By acknowledging the diversity of perspectives, we build bridges of trust and respect. We begin to understand that everyone has their own unique journey shaped by a different set of values, and that these differences enrich the world around us. Instead of reacting with surprise or discomfort to unfamiliar customs, we approach them with respect and a genuine desire to understand the stories behind them.

This deeper level of empathy not only enhances our personal relationships but also has a profound impact on how we engage in a broader, interconnected world. Whether it's through cross-cultural exchanges, collaborative work environments, or international diplomacy, cultural relativity encourages us to approach interactions with sensitivity and an appreciation for complexity. It allows us to move beyond surface-level differences and truly connect with others on a deeper, more authentic level. In embracing cultural relativity, we not only expand our worldview but also create the space for shared humanity to shine through. We learn to see people not as representatives of a particular culture but as individuals with unique experiences, dreams, and aspirations. This deeper understanding paves the way for genuine relationships, where people feel seen, heard, and valued for who they truly are, regardless of where they come from.

Ultimately, cultural relativity is not just a tool for understanding others—it's a powerful means of cultivating empathy. It encourages us to move beyond stereotypes and assumptions, offering us the chance to forge connections based on mutual respect, shared understanding, and a celebration of our differences.

Through this lens, the world becomes a more interconnected, compassionate place, where people from all walks of life can come together and form relationships that transcend cultural boundaries.

ll. Geographical Relativity:

As we've seen, cultural relativity teaches us that concepts like justice, happiness, and identity are not universal truths, but are instead shaped by the specific contexts of the societies in which we live. Similarly, geographical relativity—how our location in the world influences our worldview and values—adds another layer to this complexity. Just as cultural norms vary across societies, so too does the way we interpret and react to situations based on the place we call home. Our environment, whether it's a sprawling metropolis, a quiet rural village, or a tight-knit community, deeply impacts how we see the world and how we define ourselves within it. Geographical location doesn't just determine where we live; it shapes the very lens through which we view life. For instance, people raised in different environments— whether it's the fast-paced life of a city or the more communal atmosphere of a rural town—often have fundamentally different ways of seeing the world and understanding their roles in it. The values that are emphasized in a particular region often reflect its history, economy, and social structure.

In urban settings, where individualism and ambition are often prized, identity is shaped by one's career, personal achievements, and social mobility. Cities like New York, Tokyo, or London encourage the pursuit of personal success, with people often defining themselves by their professional accomplishments or the social circles they belong to. In these environments, personal autonomy is a central value, and the belief that individuals can "reinvent" themselves based on their own choices is widely accepted. On the other hand, rural areas often place a higher value on tradition, community, and family. Here, identity might be defined more by one's ties to the land, family heritage, or a sense of collective responsibility. A farmer in a rural community may see themselves not just as an individual, but as part of a larger, generational story—one that emphasizes hard work, continuity, and social cohesion. In these places, values like self-sufficiency, respect for nature, and loyalty to one's community are often at the forefront.

These contrasting values—individual achievement versus collective responsibility—reflect how geographical location plays a significant role in shaping worldview and identity. Our physical environment doesn't just influence how we live; it also deeply affects how we think, feel, and make decisions.

How People from Different Regions May Interpret the Same Situation Differently

Given that geographic locations create such distinct contexts, it's no surprise that people from different places might interpret the same situation or idea in vastly different ways. A single event can be seen through multiple lenses, depending on the social, economic, and historical realities of the region in which one lives.

Perceptions of Authority and Governance

Take, for example, the concept of authority. In some parts of the world, particularly in places with a history of political upheaval or colonial oppression, authority figures may be viewed with deep suspicion. In many parts of Latin America, the Middle East, and Africa, where distrust of governmental institutions runs deep due to historical abuses of power, people may perceive government actions as oppressive rather than protective. This perception stems from a long history of authoritarian regimes or colonial control, where people were often subjugated by those in power.

Contrastingly, in countries with long-established democratic institutions—like the Scandinavian countries, Canada, or parts of Western Europe—the relationship with authority tends to be more trusting and collaborative. Citizens in these regions are often more likely to see government institutions as benevolent or as systems in place to ensure fairness and justice. In this context, the same act—say, a law being enforced by the police—might be viewed as either an assurance of order or an example of government overreach, depending on the region in which it occurs.

Gender Roles and Family Dynamics

Geography also plays a significant role in shaping how gender roles and family dynamics are perceived.

In rural or conservative areas of countries like India, Egypt, or rural Southern United States, gender roles may be more strictly defined. In these communities, the expectation may be that women focus primarily on homemaking, child-rearing, and family care, while men are seen as the primary breadwinners. In these regions, a woman choosing to pursue a career outside the home might be seen as disruptive to traditional values or even as a sign of social rebellion.

In contrast, in more urbanized and progressive regions, such as in much of Western Europe, North America, or urban centers in East Asia, gender roles are often more fluid, and women's participation in the workforce is generally seen as normal and even empowering. The same choice—a woman pursuing a career—might be interpreted as a reflection of independence and self-empowerment, rather than a challenge to family dynamics. This disparity in interpretation highlights how geographical location affects societal norms and expectations, influencing how individuals make choices and how those choices are viewed by others.

Approaches to Conflict Resolution

Another example of geographical relativity can be seen in the way people from different regions approach conflict resolution. In countries like Japan or South Korea, where social harmony and saving face are deeply ingrained values, people are generally taught to avoid direct confrontation. The emphasis is often on maintaining harmony and resolving issues through indirect communication. Public disagreements or overt displays of anger can be seen as a loss of dignity, not just for the individuals involved but for the community as a whole.

In contrast, in more individualistic cultures, such as in the United States or parts of Western Europe, direct confrontation is often viewed as a productive and necessary part of conflict resolution. In these contexts, expressing one's grievances openly is seen as a way to clear the air and find solutions. What might be considered a constructive disagreement in one society could be seen as an unacceptable breach of social harmony in another. These contrasting approaches to conflict show how geographical location—shaped by culture, history, and societal values—can lead to vastly different interpretations of the same situation.

Geography and Identity Formation

Beyond how we perceive the world, geography plays a vital role in shaping our sense of self and belonging. For someone raised in a bustling city, identity might be tied to a sense of personal freedom, opportunity, and independence. The fast pace of urban life often encourages individuals to define themselves through their career, social status, or achievements. In cities, where diversity is celebrated, people might feel empowered to carve out their own identity, influenced by a variety of cultural, ethnic, and social influences. A person raised in New York, London, or Tokyo might see themselves as part of a larger global community, defined by their personal choices rather than any single cultural heritage. On the other hand, individuals raised in rural or less urbanized regions may experience identity in terms of continuity, community, and tradition. In such areas, one's sense of self is often linked to family, the land, or long-established customs. A person raised in a small village or countryside might place more value on shared history and local connections, viewing themselves as part of a larger social fabric that has existed for generations. The ties to family and community can create a sense of identity that is more collective than individual, with social roles and expectations shaping how one understands themselves.

This difference in how identity is formed based on geographic location reflects the diversity of human experience. It shows that our sense of self is not just shaped by individual experiences, but by the broader cultural, social, and geographic environments that surround us. Geography not only influences how we interact with the world—it also shapes who we are, how we define our roles in society, and how we relate to others. Just as cultural relativity challenges us to see that values like justice, happiness, and identity are relative to our cultural upbringing, geographical relativity reminds us that our environment—where we live—profoundly shapes how we understand and interact with the world. Whether we come from a bustling city or a quiet rural town, our geographical context affects everything from our worldview to the way we handle conflict, form relationships, and define our identities. Understanding this geographical influence helps us appreciate the many diverse ways in which people experience life. It teaches us that there is no single way to see the world or interpret the same situation—there are as many perspectives as there are places, each shaped by the unique characteristics of its environment. This deeper understanding fosters empathy and opens up a richer, more inclusive view of humanity, one that respects the diverse ways people across the globe navigate their lives.

As we've explored, geographical location plays a fundamental role in shaping our worldview, values, and behaviors. The environment we inhabit—whether it's a dense urban center or a quiet rural village—does not simply affect the way we live; it influences the very way we think, interact with others, and make sense of the world. In fact, geography plays a profound role in shaping language, behavior, and social norms, all of which contribute to our sense of identity. Our unique geography doesn't just give us a place to live; it provides the context within which we form our understanding of ourselves and the world around us.

The Role of Geography in Shaping Language, Behavior, and Social Norms

One of the most immediate and noticeable ways geography influences us is through language. The words we use, the dialects we speak, and even the nonverbal communication we engage in are deeply tied to the places we come from. For example, people raised in the American South may use expressions like "y'all" or "bless your heart," while someone from New York might favor directness and quick speech patterns. Similarly, the use of regional accents, colloquialisms, and even slang can serve as a marker of identity, signifying where we're from and shaping the way we relate to others. But language is not just about words; it's also about how we communicate. The role of nonverbal communication varies significantly across cultures and geographies. In some regions, people use a lot of gestures or physical touch to convey warmth and emotion, while in other places, personal space and restrained gestures are more highly valued. For instance, in Mediterranean or Latin American cultures, people may express themselves with open arms, frequent touch, and lively facial expressions. In contrast, Northern European and East Asian cultures might place more emphasis on modesty, reserve, and maintaining a respectful distance.

These geographical differences in language and communication patterns influence behavior. For example, in some cultures, expressing disagreement directly is seen as a sign of confidence and clarity, while in others, it's considered disrespectful or disruptive. In places where maintaining harmony and avoiding confrontation is valued—such as in many East Asian countries—individuals are often taught to use indirect language to resolve disagreements, thus preserving social relationships. Conversely, in cultures like the United States or many European nations, where directness is often appreciated, open confrontation might be viewed as necessary for clear communication and problem-solving.

Similarly, geographical location plays a huge role in shaping social norms—those unwritten rules about how we should behave, what is considered acceptable, and how to relate to others. In more collective societies, such as in parts of Africa, India, or Latin America, there is often an emphasis on community, family bonds, and social responsibility. The well-being of the group tends to take precedence over individual desires, and social norms encourage conformity and cooperation. For instance, in many Asian cultures, the concept of "saving face" is important, where avoiding shame or embarrassment for oneself or others is a key social goal. This deeply affects how individuals interact in social settings, especially in situations involving conflict or disagreement. On the other hand, in individualistic societies—like those in much of Western Europe or North America—the social norm leans more toward personal freedom, individual rights, and self-expression. People from these regions may be more likely to prioritize personal goals and achievements over group consensus, and societal expectations often encourage standing out or asserting one's individuality. This can manifest in everything from the ways people approach work-life balance to the value placed on creative expression or career success.

Identity and Geography: A Deep Connection

Our sense of identity, in many ways, is intimately tied to the place we come from. Where we are raised—what kind of neighborhood, city, or country we grow up in—plays a pivotal role in shaping not only the person we become, but how we view our place in the world. For many people, the idea of "home" is a central component of who they are. It's not just a physical space; it's an emotional and cultural touchstone, deeply embedded in our identities. For example, someone raised in a coastal town might feel a deep connection to the sea, valuing outdoor activities like surfing or fishing, and developing a worldview that is closely tied to nature and the rhythms of the ocean. Someone from a mountainous region might feel a similar bond to the land, viewing their identity through the lens of outdoor adventures or traditional ways of living that are shaped by the terrain. In both cases, their geographic environment shapes not only their daily lives but their core values, attitudes, and beliefs about the world. Even the rhythm of life—whether it's the slow pace of rural areas or the fast-moving energy of urban centers—contributes to a person's self-image. For individuals living in major metropolitan areas, identity may be shaped by exposure to a diverse range of cultures, ideas, and experiences. In cities like London, New York, or Berlin, where multiple cultural influences converge, identity can become more fluid, shaped by interaction with people from around the globe. These individuals might identify not just with a particular culture or nationality, but with an urban identity that is cosmopolitan and global in scope. This creates a sense of belonging that transcends geography, allowing for a multifaceted sense of self that reflects the diversity and openness inherent in metropolitan life. However, geographical ties can also shape identity in ways that create strong feelings of attachment and loyalty to one's place of origin. In rural or small-town settings, identity may be more strongly connected to family history, local traditions, and the continuity of community life. Here, identity can feel more anchored in the land and in the social relationships that have been nurtured over generations. People from such areas may feel a deep sense of pride in their local community, seeing themselves as part of a collective narrative that stretches back through time.

Mobility and Exposure: Broadening Perspective

While geography strongly influences our sense of identity, mobility—whether it's through travel, migration, or exposure to different places—can broaden our perspectives, challenging our ingrained ways of thinking. When individuals leave their familiar environments and immerse themselves in new geographic and cultural contexts, they are often forced to reconsider their assumptions and beliefs. This exposure can be transformative, allowing individuals to see their own cultural norms as just one of many possible ways to live and think. For instance, someone who has lived their whole life in a rural village might gain a new understanding of city life, perhaps learning to appreciate the opportunities for innovation, social mobility, and anonymity that come with urban living. Similarly, someone raised in a cosmopolitan city might travel to a remote village and come to value the close-knit sense of community, the deep connection to the land, or the slower pace of life. As mobility increases in the modern world—whether through immigration, travel, or digital connectivity—people are increasingly exposed to different geographical contexts, allowing them to see the world through a broader lens. This exposure encourages empathy, as individuals recognize that the norms and values that shape them are not universal. Instead, they are shaped by specific historical, cultural, and geographical conditions. As people move from one place to another, they begin to understand that there is no single "correct" way to live or think; rather, there are multiple perspectives that are all valid in their own context. The act of moving between different geographical locations doesn't just expand our physical horizons; it also challenges and enriches our sense of self. We begin to see ourselves not as static beings shaped by the place we were born, but as dynamic individuals whose identities can be shaped by multiple experiences and influences. This fluidity of identity is a powerful reminder that, while geography deeply influences who we are, we are not bound by it. Instead, we have the ability to redefine ourselves through exposure to new places and cultures, expanding our worldview and embracing the diversity of human experience.

Geography, in its many forms, shapes not only the places where we live but also the very core of who we are. From language to social norms, to the behaviors we adopt and the identities we form, our geographic location is a powerful force in the creation of our worldview. Yet, as we move through life and encounter new environments—whether through travel, migration, or exposure to different cultures— we are reminded that our sense of identity is not fixed. It is fluid, shaped by the places we come from, but also by the places we go and the people we meet along the way. Embracing this geographic relativity allows us to appreciate the diverse ways in which people experience the world, and opens up opportunities for greater empathy, understanding, and connection. It teaches us that our sense of self is not defined solely by where we are from, but by the broader tapestry of experiences, places, and people we encounter throughout our lives.

lll. Perspectival Relativity:

Continuing from the idea that our experiences, cultural contexts, and geographies shape who we are, the concept of *perspectival relativity*—the recognition that everyone perceives the world through their unique vantage point—is another essential piece of the puzzle. This idea invites us to acknowledge the subjectivity of human perception, revealing that our views on any given situation are profoundly influenced by our personal experiences, biases, and understanding. It challenges us to think beyond our own perspectives, considering that every person sees the world differently, even when faced with the same event or scenario. This understanding leads to deeper empathy and more meaningful interactions, offering us a way to connect more genuinely with people from all walks of life.

The Subjectivity of Human Perception

At its core, *perspectival relativity* underscores that our view of the world is never neutral; it is always filtered through our personal lens. These lenses are shaped by everything from the family we were born into, the education we received, the cultural norms we were taught, and even the media we consume. Because of these factors, each of us comes to any given situation with a pre-existing framework that affects how we interpret the world around us. For instance, imagine two people watching the same documentary about climate change. One person, who grew up in an environment deeply affected by environmental changes, might view the film with urgency, interpreting it as a critical call for action. This person may feel a personal connection to the issue, driven by their own experiences of wildfires, flooding, or other climate-related disruptions. Meanwhile, another person, who has lived in an area where climate change has not yet been felt as intensely, might see the documentary more as an intellectual topic, perhaps even questioning the degree of urgency. Both individuals are watching the same film, but their personal histories and experiences shape how they absorb and process the information. These differences in perception aren't just limited to abstract topics like climate change—they also affect how we understand human behavior, politics, history, and social interactions. For example, someone who grew up in a politically conservative household may see a public policy aimed at social welfare as a necessary tool for equality and opportunity, while someone raised in a liberal household might view the same policy as a crucial step toward justice and fairness. The differences in interpretation arise not because one person is "right" and the other is "wrong," but because their frameworks for understanding the world are different, influenced by their backgrounds, values, and personal histories.

How Two People Can Witness the Same Event and Interpret It Differently

The concept of *perspectival relativity* becomes particularly apparent when we consider how two people can witness the same event and come away with completely different interpretations of what transpired. These divergent interpretations are not the result of any intentional deceit or misunderstanding, but rather the natural consequence of seeing the world through distinct subjective lenses. Consider, for instance, a simple everyday situation: two people watching a disagreement between a boss and an employee. To one person, the boss's tone might seem harsh and controlling, perhaps interpreting the exchange as an example of power dynamics gone wrong. The other person, however, may interpret the boss's actions as firm but fair, viewing the employee as someone who needs constructive criticism to improve their performance. Both people are witnessing the same event—the same words spoken, the same body language—but their interpretations differ based on their personal beliefs about authority, work culture, or past experiences with similar situations.

One person might have had an authoritarian boss in the past who belittled employees, and thus perceives the situation through that lens of negativity, perhaps even seeing it as a microcosm of a larger systemic issue. On the other hand, the other person might have had mentors or supervisors who used tough love or direct communication to motivate their team, and thus interprets the scene as a form of professional guidance. In both cases, each individual interprets the same set of actions in a vastly different way. These subjective interpretations of reality are shaped by the individual's history, biases, and personal context. In many ways, *perspectival relativity* helps us understand why two people can have completely different takes on the same event, even when the facts are identical. Their conclusions are not necessarily wrong or right; they are merely different perspectives based on the different lenses through which they view the world. This makes clear that our understanding of events is always partial and incomplete, shaped by our unique experiences and points of reference.

The Importance of Acknowledging Each Perspective

Recognizing that every person's perspective is shaped by their own experiences, beliefs, and biases is a crucial step toward fostering deeper empathy and understanding. It helps us understand that no single viewpoint can be considered the *absolute truth*. Instead, truth is often multifaceted and complex, with each perspective offering a valuable piece of the overall picture. Take, for example, a political debate between two individuals with opposing views on an issue. Rather than dismissing the other person's perspective as misguided or wrong, recognizing *perspectival relativity* allows us to see that their position is shaped by their own set of life experiences, values, and concerns. Someone who advocates for stricter immigration policies might do so based on a sense of national security or a belief in the rule of law, while someone who supports open borders may be motivated by compassion, human rights, or a belief in the global interconnectedness of modern society. These differing perspectives are not necessarily irreconcilable, but they reflect different priorities and interpretations of what is fair, just, and necessary. The key to a productive conversation in such situations is not to "win" or to force someone to adopt our viewpoint, but to create space for mutual understanding. Acknowledging that each perspective is valid within its own context does not mean that all viewpoints are equally effective or that every opinion should be equally respected in every circumstance. It means that, within the context of a person's experiences and worldview, their perspective is legitimate, even if it differs from ours. This does not mean that all opinions are equally informed or equally grounded in truth. There are certainly perspectives that are harmful, misguided, or based on misinformation. But even in such cases, understanding why a person holds a certain view—what experiences, fears, or beliefs led them to that viewpoint—allows for a more meaningful and empathetic dialogue. It shifts the conversation away from attacking the person and toward understanding the motivations behind their beliefs, creating space for the possibility of constructive change.

How Understanding Different Perspectives Leads to More Meaningful and Constructive Interactions

Understanding that all perspectives are shaped by personal context—and acknowledging that no single viewpoint holds the absolute truth—has profound implications for how we interact with others. It encourages us to approach others with curiosity rather than judgment, and to engage in conversations with an open mind, ready to listen as much as we speak. When we approach interactions with an awareness of *perspectival relativity*, we are more likely to engage in thoughtful, meaningful conversations. Instead of assuming that people who disagree with us are wrong, we can ask ourselves what factors shaped their views. We might ask: What life experiences have they had that led them to see the world in this way? What values or cultural influences have informed their perspective? What fears or hopes do they have that might shape the way they interpret the world?

Such questions open up space for empathy, even in situations where we might strongly disagree. Take, for example, the contentious issue of gun control in the United States. Two people—one who supports the right to own firearms and another who advocates for stricter gun laws—may seem to be at an impasse, with each side holding firmly to their views. However, if each person understands that the other's perspective is shaped by deeply held beliefs about personal freedom, safety, or historical experience, they can begin to find common ground. One person may be motivated by a deep sense of individual autonomy and the belief in the constitutional right to bear arms, while the other may be focused on reducing violence and ensuring public safety. These perspectives are not inherently incompatible; they are just framed differently, shaped by different experiences and values. By understanding this, the conversation becomes less about attacking the other person's position and more about finding ways to address both people's core concerns. What shared values can they agree on? How can they build a conversation that respects both the right to personal freedom and the need for collective safety? Recognizing that each perspective is valid within its own context can pave the way for deeper, more constructive discussions that move beyond polarized positions and into more nuanced, thoughtful solutions.

The recognition of *perspectival relativity*—the subjectivity of human perception—encourages us to understand that everyone sees the world from a unique vantage point, shaped by their individual experiences, biases, and values. This understanding reveals that our perceptions are never purely objective; they are always filtered through our personal lens. As a result, two people witnessing the same event can interpret it in vastly different ways, depending on their own backgrounds, worldviews, and emotional states. The key to navigating this diversity of perspectives is acknowledging that each viewpoint is valid within its own context. When we approach the world with an openness to different perspectives, we foster empathy, promote deeper understanding, and create the conditions for more meaningful and constructive interactions. In a world where disagreements and misunderstandings are inevitable, recognizing *perspectival relativity* can help us build bridges between people, communities, and cultures. It invites us to move beyond the confines of our own views and engage with others in a more thoughtful, compassionate way—ultimately broadening our own understanding of the world and making us more connected to the richness of human experience.

IV. Contextual Relativity: Meaning Defined by Situation

As we continue to explore the multifaceted nature of human perception, we arrive at *contextual relativity*— the profound understanding that the meaning and significance of actions, words, or behaviors are not fixed or universal, but are deeply influenced by the specific context in which they occur. The context in which something happens—the historical, social, emotional, and even physical circumstances surrounding an event—plays a pivotal role in shaping its interpretation. Philosophically, this concept invites us to question the objectivity of our judgments and to appreciate the fluid, dynamic nature of meaning in human experience. In essence, the full meaning of any phenomenon is contingent upon the situation in which it arises, and without understanding this context, our judgments can be incomplete, superficial, or misguided.

The Influence of Context on Meaning

In everyday life, we often encounter situations where the meaning of a word, action, or gesture is entirely dependent on the context in which it occurs. What might seem like a harmless joke in one setting could be perceived as offensive or inappropriate in another. A phrase that expresses sympathy or encouragement in one scenario might come across as patronizing or hollow in a different one. The same action can evoke varying responses depending on the time, place, and social environment in which it is performed.

Consider, for example, the simple act of a person saying "I love you." In the context of a romantic relationship, these words carry deep emotional significance, representing affection, commitment, and intimacy. However, the same phrase, when said by a parent to a child, might convey warmth and nurturing, but with a very different kind of intimacy—one that is more protective and caring rather than romantic. The words "I love you" carry a vastly different meaning in each context, shaped by the relationship between the speaker and the listener, the shared history, and the emotional tone. Similarly, the same words might sound hollow or insincere if spoken in a context where they are expected to be backed by tangible actions, such as in a professional setting or a situation where trust has been broken.

This example illustrates how meaning is not an intrinsic property of words or actions themselves, but rather is shaped by the relational and situational factors surrounding them. We interpret the same words, gestures, or behaviors in dramatically different ways depending on the context in which they are delivered. Meaning, then, becomes a dynamic and context-dependent phenomenon, rather than something fixed and absolute.

The Role of Historical, Social, Emotional and situational Contexts

Contextual relativity, philosophically speaking, challenges us to recognize the inseparable connection between meaning and the conditions under which an event unfolds. History, society, emotion and situation are all key elements in this equation.

Historical Context: History is one of the most powerful forces that shapes meaning. What seems innocuous or neutral today can carry immense historical baggage, and words or actions from the past can take on new significance when considered within the historical context in which they arose. This is especially apparent when we look at political rhetoric, social movements, or the interpretation of past events. Consider, for example, the phrase *"The greatest country in the world."* In the United States, this phrase is frequently used in political speeches and media, and it often evokes a sense of national pride and exceptionalism. Yet, to someone from a historically oppressed community within that same country, the phrase may carry a different connotation. For a Native American or African American, the idea of "greatness" might be entwined with historical memories of genocide, slavery, and systemic inequality, making the statement not a source of pride, but of tension or discomfort. The meaning of the phrase changes depending on the historical context of those who hear it. Similarly, historical events are often interpreted in radically different ways depending on one's perspective and the context in which the interpretation occurs. A historical figure such as Christopher Columbus, once widely celebrated for "discovering" the Americas, is now increasingly viewed through a critical lens due to the context of colonial violence and exploitation that followed his voyages. The very same historical figure can be a symbol of adventure and discovery in one context, and a symbol of oppression and genocide in another. These examples highlight how our understanding of events, language, and actions is not isolated from time, but is deeply embedded in the history that precedes them. Meaning, therefore, is shaped by the narratives we inherit from the past.

Social Context: The social context in which an interaction takes place is equally significant. Social norms, cultural values, and power dynamics influence how actions and words are received and interpreted. Social context encompasses everything from societal expectations, gender roles, racial and ethnic identities, and even the economic status of individuals. A single word or gesture might evoke different emotions or interpretations depending on who is involved and the broader societal structures that frame the situation. For example, a simple touch on the arm or a pat on the back might be interpreted as friendly and supportive in one social context, such as among close friends or family members. In a different context—say, in the workplace or a public setting—the same touch could be viewed as inappropriate or even an infringement on personal boundaries. Social norms regarding touch vary dramatically across cultures, and even within a given culture, they shift depending on the circumstances. Similarly, *class differences* play a crucial role in interpreting meaning. A phrase like *"Let them eat cake"*—attributed to Marie Antoinette, the Queen of France—might initially be read as a symbol of royal indifference to the plight of the poor. However, depending on the social context in which it is spoken, its meaning might shift. In a post-revolutionary society, the phrase would likely be considered a symbol of aristocratic decadence and oppression, whereas in a modern context, it might be seen as a critique of wealth inequality and the detachment of the elite from the struggles of ordinary people.

The power dynamics between individuals also affect the interpretation of actions or words. A joke made by a superior to a subordinate may be heard as humorous or even bonding in certain contexts, but in another, it could be interpreted as condescending or even coercive. A statement made by a person with power can carry a different weight than the same statement made by someone without it. For example, a wealthy person's comment about how "hard it is to manage their money" might be seen as tone-deaf or arrogant by someone living in poverty. Social class, power, and privilege are crucial elements in understanding how context shapes meaning.

Emotional Context: While historical and social contexts define much of how we interpret events, the emotional context in which something occurs also profoundly affects our understanding. Emotions are not mere reactions; they color how we perceive everything around us. A person who is feeling anxious or depressed might interpret neutral or even positive actions negatively, while someone who is feeling joyful might interpret the same actions as uplifting or encouraging. Take, for example, a situation where a friend sends a text message saying, *"Are you okay?"* In one emotional context, the recipient might see this as a sign of genuine concern and care. However, in another emotional context—say, if the person has just had an argument with their friend—the same message might be interpreted as patronizing or condescending, even if it was not intended that way. Emotions influence our perceptions in subtle, often unconscious ways, shaping how we interpret what others say and do. Similarly, the emotional state of an individual will affect their interpretation of humor. A joke that would be laughed at during a relaxed, friendly gathering might be perceived as harmful or malicious if told during a time of emotional vulnerability or stress. In the context of heightened emotions—whether positive or negative—the meaning of words and actions becomes more intensely felt and, consequently, more open to subjective interpretation.

Situational Context: Finally, the immediate situational context plays a significant role in shaping meaning. This includes the specifics of the moment— where the interaction is taking place, the people involved, and what is happening at that particular point in time. For example, a person who laughs loudly at a joke in a quiet, formal setting may be seen as rude or disruptive, while the same laughter in a casual, social gathering may be interpreted as an expression of enjoyment and camaraderie. The immediate environment, including both physical space and social atmosphere, alters the way actions and words are received.

Take another example: a person who interrupts during a conversation might be seen as rude or disrespectful in a formal meeting, but the same interruption might be welcomed in a brainstorming session or an informal discussion, where it may be considered a sign of enthusiasm or a desire to contribute. Situational context influences not only how we interpret the behavior of others but also how we shape our own responses.

Examples of Contextual Relativity in Action

There are countless examples in everyday life where the same action, phrase, or behavior is interpreted differently depending on the context. Let us explore a few that illuminate the importance of context in shaping meaning:

- **Humor and Offense:** A joke that is received with laughter in a group of close friends might be seen as deeply offensive in a formal or professional setting. Consider the phrase "That's so gay!" In a group of friends where this phrase is used in a joking, light-hearted way, it may not be meant with any ill intent. However, in a different context, especially with someone who has experienced discrimination or marginalization due to their sexual orientation, the phrase could be interpreted as homophobic or disrespectful. The same words, depending on the situation in which they are spoken, may carry vastly different meanings. Understanding this context is essential before passing judgment on whether something is humorous or offensive.

- **Social Norms and Cultural Sensitivity:** A person may offer a firm handshake as a sign of respect and friendliness in one culture, but in another culture, a handshake might be seen as too forward or impolite. In some cultures, physical touch is avoided, and a bow or a verbal greeting may carry more significance than any physical gesture. Similarly, while making direct eye contact may signify honesty or confidence in many Western cultures, in certain Asian cultures, avoiding direct eye contact may be a sign of respect and deference. These differences underscore the significance of social context in shaping how actions or behaviors are perceived.

- **Behavior in Times of Crisis:** In the midst of a crisis, a person's behavior might be interpreted in ways that are drastically different from how it would be understood in a calm, everyday setting. Imagine a person who begins to shout in a public space. In a non-crisis setting, their behavior might be viewed as rude, disruptive, or aggressive. However, in a situation where the person is responding to a sudden emergency, such as an evacuation or a call for help, the same behavior might be seen as a necessary and urgent reaction. The context— whether it's a routine day or a moment of crisis—changes the interpretation of the person's actions.

These examples emphasize how easily meaning can shift based on the surrounding circumstances. It is not enough to observe an event in isolation; we must always take into account the broader context in order to truly understand its meaning and significance.

The Philosophical Importance of Contextual Relativity

From a philosophical standpoint, the recognition of *contextual relativity* invites us to reconsider how we make judgments about the world and about each other. It challenges the traditional notion that meaning can be distilled into objective, unchanging truths, independent of the circumstances in which they occur. Instead, it compels us to acknowledge that all human actions and expressions are embedded in a web of contexts—historical, social, emotional, and situational—that shape their meaning.

This philosophical perspective has profound ethical implications. In ethics, *contextualism* argues that the morality of an action cannot be fully understood without considering the specific situation in which it occurs. For example, the ethics of lying depend significantly on the context in which the lie is told. Lying to protect someone from harm might be seen as morally acceptable in certain contexts (such as lying to protect a person's safety), while lying for personal gain might be viewed as unethical in another. Without understanding the full context of an action, our judgments may be superficial or incomplete, failing to account for the nuanced moral complexities of human behavior. Similarly, *contextualism* in communication theory emphasizes that meaning is shaped not only by the words we say but also by the situation in which they are said, the relationships between the speakers, and the cultural norms at play. This means that understanding language requires more than a literal interpretation of words; it demands an awareness of the context in which the language is used and the social dynamics that inform its meaning. In essence, *contextual relativity* challenges the notion of universal, one-size-fits-all judgments. It teaches us that understanding requires us to look beyond surface appearances and to explore the underlying conditions that shape meaning. In doing so, we cultivate more thoughtful, empathetic ways of engaging with others and a deeper understanding of the complexities of human experience.

Contextual relativity is a reminder that meaning is never fixed, but always contingent upon the circumstances that surround it. Words, actions, and behaviors are all understood differently depending on their historical, social, emotional, and situational contexts. As we move through the world, this understanding encourages us to adopt a more reflective and discerning approach, where we recognize the fluidity and complexity of meaning in human interactions. Philosophically, this concept compels us to approach judgment with humility and awareness, acknowledging that without a full understanding of the context in which something occurs, our conclusions are necessarily incomplete. By embracing *contextual relativity*, we cultivate a deeper empathy for the perspectives and experiences of others, and we move closer to a more nuanced and compassionate understanding of the world around us. This recognition enriches our ability to navigate the complexity of human life, fostering more thoughtful, compassionate, and ethical interactions in an increasingly interconnected world.

V. Temporal Relativity: The Influence of Time on Perception

As we delve deeper into the nature of human perception, *temporal relativity* introduces another layer of complexity—one that acknowledges how the passage of time fundamentally alters the way we perceive events, people, and decisions. Much like the geographical, cultural, and contextual lenses we've discussed, time too serves as a powerful lens through which our experiences are refracted, reshaping our understanding of the world and ourselves as we move through it. Time does not simply mark the linear progression of moments; it molds and refines our perceptions, turning once fixed understandings into fluid, ever-evolving interpretations.

The Passage of Time and the Shifting Perception of Events

The notion that time alters perception is immediately evident in how our understanding of events changes as we reflect on them. The way we interpret an experience is not the same in the present moment as it is years later, and this shift often reveals deeper truths about the nature of human perception. Time does not simply pass without consequence; it reshapes how we make meaning of our lives.

For instance, consider a moment of failure or rejection that initially seemed devastating. At the time, it might have felt like a personal crisis, one that defined the trajectory of your life. But as time moves forward, the same event may be reframed as a valuable lesson, a catalyst for growth that led to new opportunities or a better understanding of your own strength. The pain of the moment diminishes, but in its place, there is a new understanding of how that event fit into the broader story of your life. The same situation, in retrospect, carries a different significance—one shaped by the wisdom gained in the intervening time.

This is a core idea in *temporal relativity*: that the meaning of our experiences is not set in stone. Time allows us to reinterpret the events in our lives, often transforming what was once perceived as a misstep into an essential part of our personal evolution. The passage of time provides the emotional distance needed to see the bigger picture, allowing us to connect the dots in ways that were not possible in the heat of the moment.

Memory and the Fluidity of Past Experiences

Our memories of the past are also deeply influenced by time. The human mind does not record events with perfect clarity; rather, it stores impressions that shift over time, adapting to new contexts and understandings. As we accumulate more experiences, the meaning of precious moments is often rewritten, sometimes even altering the way we feel about them. Take, for example, the childhood memory of a family vacation. At the time, it might have been a moment of pure joy and excitement. But as an adult, you might look back and realize how those experiences were shaped by underlying family tensions or socioeconomic challenges. Your memories of that trip, once painted in broad strokes of happiness, now take on more nuance as you gain a deeper understanding of the complexities of family dynamics. Time, in this case, doesn't erase the joy you felt but allows you to see it in a new light, expanding your appreciation of what was happening beneath the surface. Similarly, as we mature, our memories of relationships also undergo transformation. A friendship or romantic relationship that was once central to our identity might, with the passage of time, fade into the background or evolve into something less significant. The way we view these relationships is continually reshaped by the different stages of our lives, as we change, grow, and develop new understandings of what we value.

This process of reframing memories is central to the idea of *temporal relativity*. It suggests that time itself is an active force in shaping how we understand the past, highlighting the fluid nature of our memories and how they are constantly being reinterpreted in the present. Our memories, then, are not static; they evolve with us, and the meaning we attribute to them shifts as we gain new perspectives.

The Concept of "Hindsight" and Its Role in Shaping Present Understanding

A key component of *temporal relativity* is the concept of hindsight—the tendency to reinterpret past events with the benefit of new knowledge or insight. In hindsight, we often see events differently than we did in the moment, shaping our understanding of the past in a way that aligns more closely with our current perspective. This phenomenon can provide clarity, but it can also lead to a distorted view of the past, one that seems overly simplified or overly deterministic. For instance, consider a decision you made years ago that seemed uncertain or full of risk at the time. Now, with the benefit of hindsight, you may view that decision as inevitable or even obvious. Hindsight offers us a sense of certainty about past actions, but it also obscures the complexity and uncertainty that existed when those decisions were made. It makes us believe that, given the knowledge we have now, we could have predicted the outcome more easily. However, this belief often disregards the fact that, in the moment, we were operating with limited information and an incomplete understanding of the consequences.

This retrospective clarity can also be both comforting and frustrating. It provides us with the opportunity to make sense of our choices, but it can also lead us to feel regret or self-doubt. The difference between how we viewed an event in the past and how we view it in the present can create a gap that reflects the distance between where we were and where we are now—a gap that often highlights how far we've come in our personal journey. Yet, there's a philosophical richness to this process. *Hindsight* suggests that meaning is not inherent in an event; rather, it is something we project onto the past from the present. Our understanding of our lives is therefore always in flux, reshaped by the experiences and insights we accumulate over time.

The Fluidity of Time and Life's Ever-Changing Meaning

As we reflect on the passage of time, *temporal relativity* challenges us to understand that meaning itself is not fixed—it shifts and evolves as we move through different phases of life. What once seemed critical may later seem trivial; what once appeared to be a failure may later be seen as a crucial learning experience. The way we perceive the world is always changing, and each phase of life offers a new lens through which we reinterpret our past and present. This fluidity of time underscores the idea that *meaning* is not static. Instead, it is deeply intertwined with the journey of personal growth and transformation. At each stage of life, we approach the world with a different set of experiences and a different understanding of who we are. This changing perspective allows us to reinterpret the significance of past experiences, shifting their meaning to align with our evolving sense of self.

For example, an individual who has recently gone through a significant life event—such as a career change or a personal loss—might look back at their earlier decisions or experiences with new understanding. The weight of those past events, once trivial or misunderstood, may now seem more significant. As we move through time, we reinterpret our own life narrative, seeing how each chapter fits into the larger story of who we are becoming. In embracing *temporal relativity*, we recognize that time is not just a marker of events—it is an active, transformative force that shapes our perceptions, our memories, and our understanding of the world. The passage of time offers us the opportunity to reinterpret the past and reframe our present understanding, allowing us to grow in wisdom and insight. This process is not just a reflection of how we change over time; it is also a profound acknowledgment of how our relationships with the past, the present, and the future are interwoven. Philosophically, *temporal relativity* invites us to appreciate the fluidity of life's meaning. As time reshapes our perceptions, we come to understand that our lives are always in the process of becoming, always subject to reinterpretation. The meaning we attach to our experiences is never fixed—it evolves, expands, and deepens with the passage of time. In this light, time becomes more than a mere measure of existence—it becomes a vehicle for self-discovery, understanding, and growth. By recognizing the influence of time on our perceptions, we open ourselves to a richer, more nuanced experience of the world, where each moment is both a reflection of who we were and a glimpse into who we are becoming.

In reflecting on the vast and intricate layers of human experience, we find that cultural, geographical, perspectival, contextual, and temporal relativity are not isolated concepts but interconnected forces that shape our understanding of the world. Each of these forms of relativity offers a unique lens through which we view and interpret our lives, and together they create a rich, multifaceted tapestry of human perception. From the cultural values that influence our beliefs to the geographical realities that define our lived experiences, from the personal perspectives that shape our decisions to the ever-evolving nature of time that reframes our memories, these forces converge to give us a complex and dynamic understanding of the world. As we embrace the interplay of these various lenses, we recognize that no single truth can encapsulate the full spectrum of human experience. Instead, there are multiple truths, each shaped by a combination of factors—culture, place, perspective, context, and time.

Adopting a relativistic worldview offers a transformative shift in how we engage with the world and others. When we acknowledge that each person's viewpoint is shaped by a unique web of influences, we open ourselves to the possibility of new experiences, perspectives, and deeper connections. Rather than approaching differences with judgment or defensiveness, we learn to approach them with curiosity and empathy, recognizing that each person's truth is as valid as our own. This willingness to step beyond our own limited perspective can lead to richer interactions, a greater understanding of others, and a more compassionate approach to life's complexities. Understanding the relativity of our perceptions allows us to see the world through a broader, more inclusive lens, where the diversity of human experience is not something to be feared or rejected, but celebrated and embraced. The lessons learned through exploring the relativity of perception remind us of the fluid, ever-changing nature of human understanding. As we reflect on the ways in which our values, beliefs, and actions are shaped by the unique combinations of cultural, geographical, personal, contextual, and temporal influences, we begin to realize that our understanding of the world is never fixed. Just as the world itself is always in flux, so too are our perceptions and interpretations of it. This realization can be both humbling and empowering. It humbles us by reminding us that we cannot claim to possess absolute truth, and it empowers us by encouraging us to approach life with openness, flexibility, and a willingness to learn.

In closing, we are reminded that the complexity of the world—its myriad truths, shaped by an endless array of influences—is what makes human experience so rich and varied. Each moment of life is seen through a distinct lens, and each person's journey is shaped by a unique combination of cultural, geographical, and temporal factors. As we embrace this complexity, we come to appreciate that there is no one-size-fits-all truth or perspective. Instead, there are many truths, many realities, and many paths to understanding. It is in this diversity, this vast spectrum of human experiences and perspectives, that the beauty of life resides. By embracing the relativistic nature of our world, we not only deepen our understanding of others, but also cultivate a richer, more compassionate understanding of ourselves and our place in the vast web of existence.

Chapter 6

The Elders

"The elders, those worn and weary souls, carry within them a truth that the young cannot yet bear to understand. They have known suffering, regret, and the quiet desperation of time slipping away, yet in their silence, there is a wisdom forged in the fires of life's harshest trials. They speak little, but in the creases of their faces, the tremble of their hands, and the weight of their eyes, they impart a lesson that the world refuses to heed—nothing is ever as it seems, and in the end, we are all prisoners of our own hearts."

The elder stands at the crossroads of wisdom and time—a figure both revered and quietly sidelined. In countless cultures, elders are seen as the stewards of knowledge, their lives etched with lessons, experiences, and insights. Their words carry the weight of centuries; their memories are the keepers of history. This perspective resonates deeply with my own childhood, where the presence of my father and his circle of friends profoundly shaped my understanding of wisdom. As a child, I often accompanied my father on bike rides to visit his friends. An exuberant extrovert, he was always seeking connections, always gathering people around him. These meetings typically took place at someone's home or a local café, where I would sit quietly in the corner, observing, listening. As restless as any child, I struggled to stay still, to engage in these conversations that seemed slow, contemplative, and removed from the quick rhythms of my own world. My father, sensing my impatience, would often turn to his friends with a knowing smile and say, "We elders have mastered the art of sitting, but children can't sit in one place." That simple comment stayed with me—a quiet reminder of the contrast between the restless energy of youth and the grounded stillness that comes with age.

Despite my youthful annoyance, those moments left a lasting mark. The wisdom shared between those elders—their stories, their reflections, their quiet exchanges—shaped me in ways I only began to understand much later. Over time, I came to recognize the value in their conversations, even in their silences. In many ways, I began to mature into what some might call an "old soul," increasingly drawn to the company of older generations rather than my peers. I found comfort in their presence, a sense of belonging in their collected wisdom. The influence of elders often transcends words, subtly shaping younger generations, guiding them in ways both seen and unseen. My own experience is a testament to how the wisdom of elders—whether imparted directly or indirectly—has the power to shape and inspire, bridging the past and the future. It reminds us that wisdom is not only passed down through formal teaching but through the quiet persistence of lived experience. But as the years pass, the body weakens. The world around the elderly transforms, sometimes in ways that make their experiences seem distant, even obsolete. While their wisdom may be rooted in timeless truths, their bodies betray them, and with it, their place in a society that prizes youth and change. In this sense, the elder occupies a contradictory space—honored for the depth of their lived experience, yet often marginalized by a world that moves ever faster, ever forward. They are, in a way, both guardians and prisoners—guardians of wisdom, perhaps, but prisoners of a world that moves on without them. The very qualities that make them revered—memory, perspective, insight—are the same ones that distance them from a culture obsessed with progress, novelty, and speed. This tension between what an elder represents and how the world perceives them runs deep. Their wisdom is timeless, yet time itself is their greatest adversary. In a culture that so often looks toward the future, the elder becomes a relic, caught between the deep past and an uncertain future. The question lingers: Do they remain the bearers of insight, or do they slowly fade into irrelevance, overshadowed by a society that values the new, the now? The elder's existence becomes a meditation on time itself—how it can enrich and deplete, how it can elevate and diminish. They stand as a reminder that wisdom and aging are not separate, but intertwined. Yet as the world continues to change, the elder's place within it becomes more fragile, uncertain. The relationship between wisdom and time is not simply philosophical; it is one of survival, adaptation, and sometimes quiet surrender. The elder, too, is a symbol of something far greater than the individual life they've lived. On the surface, they are simply a person—marked by years, moments, and memories. Their body bears the evidence of time: the wrinkles etched into their skin, the deliberate pace of their steps, the quiet wisdom in their eyes, wisdom that comes not from books but from the depth of experience. In the elder, we encounter time itself, made flesh. They are not just one person, but a living archive—a testament to a history written not in ink, but in the rhythms of daily life. Yet beyond the individual, the elder assumes a more expansive role. Across cultures, the elderly are seen as the embodiment of wisdom, continuity, and tradition. They stand as bridges between the past and the future, carrying the stories, lessons, and values that shape a community's identity. In this way, the elder is not merely a person who has lived long, but a vessel for something far larger than themselves. They bear the weight of generations, the triumphs and mistakes of those who came before them, the collective memory of their people. In their very being, they represent the unbroken chain of time—from a distant past to an uncertain future.

Yet, this symbolic role is far from fixed. The meaning we attach to elders is constantly shifting, shaped by the changing tides of culture and society. In some places, the elder is a revered sage, a figure of deep respect, sought after for guidance and insight. In others, the elderly are increasingly seen as irrelevant, even invisible—a relic of a bygone era in a world obsessed with youth, progress, and the relentless march of technology. Where once elders were the keepers of tradition, now they may be the ones who struggle to keep pace with a world that moves ever faster. This tension between the elder as an individual and as a symbol lies at the heart of their complex role. On one hand, they are a person, with their own unique life story—flawed, imperfect, and deeply human. Yet, as time passes, they also become something more: a symbol of continuity, of the unspoken wisdom that comes from having lived long enough to witness the cycles of life. They are a living paradox: at once deeply personal, and yet, through the experiences they carry, profoundly universal.

In this way, the elder serves as both an individual and a metaphor—a living testament to the passage of time, a symbol of what endures, and a reminder of what we may lose. They force us to confront the relationship between time and knowledge, between the old and the new, between memory and progress. The elder, both as a person and as an idea, asks us to reconsider how we value the past, and what we might be leaving behind as we race toward the future. The figure of the elder is inseparable from some of philosophy's most foundational themes: aging, the passage of time, wisdom, and authority. These themes, in their interplay, create a complex web of ideas that touch on both the individual experience of growing older and the broader, collective implications of time's inevitable progression. The elder becomes a living paradox, embodying the wisdom that comes with age while also confronting the limitations imposed by it.

Aging is the first theme that strikes us when we consider the elderly. Aging is often seen as a process of decline, a gradual erosion of the physical self, but it is also a profound transformation of the psyche. To grow old is to witness the changes in one's body, the gradual fading of strength, and the increasing awareness of one's mortality. Yet, aging is not merely a physical state—it is a psychological and philosophical journey. The elder embodies this tension between body and mind, between the wisdom accrued over time and the inevitable fragility that accompanies it. It forces a confrontation with the passage of life itself: How do we reconcile the fullness of a lifetime with the limitations that time imposes on us? In the elder's experience, aging becomes a reflection on life's impermanence—a process of both gaining and losing.

The Passage of Time is the invisible thread that runs through the elder's existence. Time shapes not just the elderly, but the world they inhabit, and the tension between these two forces—the person and the world—becomes a key philosophical issue. Time, with all its urgency, is a relentless force that shapes the elder's perspective. For the elderly, time can feel like both a friend and an adversary: it is the context in which wisdom is gained, but also the thing that erodes memory and experience. The elder is a living reflection of time itself—an embodiment of the fact that everything is temporary, even wisdom. Yet time, in its sweeping nature, is also a source of clarity. With age comes a sense of perspective that only the passage of time can bring. But as the world accelerates, the elder's perception of time grows increasingly out of sync with the rapidly shifting present. Time, it seems, moves differently for them than it does for the younger generations, creating a subtle tension between the old and the new.

Wisdom, as the hallmark of the elder's life, holds a special place in this philosophical framework. Wisdom is not simply knowledge or intelligence; it is the product of experience, reflection, and understanding gained over time. The elder's wisdom is a distilled form of knowledge, a quiet knowing that comes not from theoretical learning, but from lived experience—the lessons that only time can teach. But there is a question at the heart of wisdom: does it always endure? Is the wisdom of the elderly still relevant in a world that moves faster and faster, where new technologies and ideas seem to outpace everything that came before? The wisdom of the elder is born of tradition, memory, and the slow process of reflection—qualities that often seem at odds with the rapid, disposable nature of contemporary life. As the world rushes forward, the elder's wisdom can feel like a relic, a fading echo of a time when the past had more weight than the future. The question, then, becomes: Is wisdom tied to the past, or does it evolve with time?

Authority is perhaps the most complex theme in relation to the elderly. Traditionally, elders have held authority because of their age, their accumulated wisdom, and their connection to history. Their authority is quiet, not based on power or dominance, but on experience and survival. In many societies, elders are the ones to whom others turn for guidance, their voices representing the collective knowledge of a community or family. But authority is fluid, and as society changes, so too does the way we view authority itself. In today's fast-paced world, where innovation and novelty are prized, the elder's authority can seem less certain. The authority they once held through experience and tradition is often questioned, especially when it conflicts with the new ways of thinking and being that come with each generation. The elder's authority is also challenged by their very vulnerability—after all, how can one be seen as an authority when they are marked by the fragility of age? The elder is both the bearer of authority and a reminder of the limitations that age brings with it. Together, these themes—aging, the passage of time, wisdom, and authority—create a rich and intricate portrait of the elder as a philosophical figure. The elder exists at the crossroads of time and knowledge, embodying both the depth of lived experience and the fragility that time brings. Their life is a reflection of the tension between the past and the future, between what is timeless and what is fleeting. And in the elder's experience, we are reminded that while time may erode the body, it also has the power to deepen understanding and sharpen perspective. The elder's wisdom is not just a product of years, but of the relationship between time and experience—an ongoing dialogue between what is lost and what endures.

There comes a point, often in the restless hum of modern life, when we ask ourselves: *What do elders really offer us now?* Are they the treasured bearers of wisdom, or are they merely relics of a time when the world moved slower, when traditions were stronger, and when authority was rooted in experience rather than innovation? In a world that relentlessly chases progress, the question of what value elders hold is no longer easily answered.

The elder, once seen as the irreplaceable vessel of ancestral knowledge, now often finds themselves at odds with the fast-paced, ever-evolving landscape of contemporary society. What was once considered time-honed wisdom now sometimes feels out of place in an age that values immediacy and novelty over reflection and continuity. The quick swipe, the algorithmic solution, the speed of digital connectivity—these things have fundamentally altered how we experience the world and how we define expertise. In this world, the slow and deliberate thought of the elderly can feel outdated, even irrelevant.

Yet, to dismiss the elder as a mere relic is to overlook the depth and breadth of their lived experience. There is a quality in the elder's wisdom that cannot be replicated by books or computers, something that only comes from years of navigating life's complexities. In the stories they tell—the subtle shifts in tone, the pauses, the way their eyes light up when recalling moments of joy or sorrow—there is a truth that cuts through time. Their knowledge is not abstract; it is grounded in the messy, unpredictable realities of living. The elder has lived through what the younger generation may only read about in history books.

They have weathered changes—social, political, personal—that have shaped the very fabric of who they are. And in this way, they offer a kind of knowledge that is not simply academic, but deeply human. Yet, even as we recognize this, we must acknowledge that *time itself* is a double-edged sword. The wisdom of an elder is not immune to the erosion of relevance. As technology advances, as new generations reframe the world, much of what the elders know may seem out of step with the present. The traditional ways of understanding life, passed down through generations, may seem incompatible with the ideals of innovation, efficiency, and instant gratification that dominate today's culture. In this regard, the elder can begin to feel like a ghost—a figure who represents a bygone era, one that no longer holds sway in a world obsessed with what's next. The questions they raise may be seen as anachronistic, the lessons they impart as outdated.

But this begs the question: Is wisdom only valuable if it can be immediately applied? Are the things that time has taught the elderly worth less because they do not fit neatly into the fast-paced, ever-changing demands of contemporary life? Perhaps it is precisely in their slowness, in their deep engagement with the past, that the elder offers us something we cannot get elsewhere: a kind of permanence, a reminder that not everything in life can be hurried or digitized. Elders also embody a connection to a time before the present, a continuity that anchors us to the foundations upon which modernity is built. In a world that often seems adrift, their lived experience offers stability. They are the storytellers, the ones who have seen the long arc of history and can share its patterns and lessons. In that sense, they are not simply custodians of history, but also of hope—a reminder that the present moment, though fleeting, is part of a much larger human story. In the end, the question of whether elders are wisdom-bearers or relics of the past depends not on what they *offer* but on what we are willing to receive. Are we open to learning from lives that have seen the world change, or are we too enamored by the bright new promises of the future to acknowledge the value in the lived experiences of those who have already traversed many of the paths we are only now beginning to walk? The elder's true value may lie in their ability to offer perspective, to ask us questions we have forgotten to ask, and to remind us that wisdom is not about speed, but about depth. Whether we see them as bearers of wisdom or relics of a bygone era is less a judgment on them than a reflection of our own willingness to slow down, listen, and truly understand.

Wisdom is a quality we often associate with age, as if the two are inseparable—like the grains of sand in an hourglass, one slowly building up, the other slipping away. We have long believed that with the passage of time comes the sharpening of insight, the deepening of understanding. The elder, with their silver hair and lined face, becomes the living embodiment of this truth, their wisdom seemingly etched into every wrinkle, their perspective a reflection of a life fully lived. But is wisdom truly linked to age? Or is it an illusion, a cultural construct that elevates experience over the inherent qualities of knowing?

There is an undeniable appeal in the idea that wisdom comes naturally with age. The elder, as the bearer of accumulated knowledge, becomes a symbol of time's ability to carve out understanding from the raw material of experience. The longer one lives, the more they witness, learn, and process—the idea goes. In this view, wisdom is a byproduct of sheer exposure to life's complexities, its trials and triumphs, its heartbreaks and triumphs. The elder, having seen many seasons of life, is presumed to have distilled the essence of what is important, what endures, and what is fleeting. But this belief, so deeply embedded in many cultures, raises an uncomfortable question: Does time automatically confer wisdom, or is it possible to age without growing wise? Is wisdom simply a matter of surviving long enough, or does it require a certain kind of engagement with life? The elder who has lived long yet remains set in their ways, resistant to change, unreflective of the past—can they be said to be wise? Age, after all, does not guarantee introspection or growth. One can live a long life without ever fully grappling with the deeper questions of existence. The elder who repeats the same mistakes, who fails to learn from their experiences, challenges the very notion that wisdom is a natural consequence of age.

On the other hand, there are those who age with grace, their minds growing sharper, their hearts more open, their understanding of the world deepening as the years unfold. In this case, wisdom is not simply the result of time's passing, but of time *well-lived*. It comes from reflection, from the willingness to learn from both the mistakes and the triumphs. It is an active process, a continual cultivation of self-awareness and compassion, not a passive outcome of years lived. Thus, the paradox of wisdom becomes clear: *Is wisdom inherently tied to age, or is it something that can emerge independently of it?* Age may offer the context, the canvas on which wisdom can be painted, but it does not guarantee the art. Wisdom is not simply the accumulation of years; it is the ability to distill meaning from those years, to integrate them into a deeper understanding of the self and the world. It is the result of attention, reflection, and the capacity to adapt to the ever-changing tides of life. This paradox creates a complex relationship between the elder and wisdom. The elder becomes a paradox themselves: a living representation of both what is gained and what is lost with time. On one hand, they are the repository of history, the carriers of experience; on the other, they are vulnerable to the erosion of memory, the narrowing of perspective, and the rigidity that can come with age. Their wisdom is often the result of overcoming hardship, surviving tragedy, and learning to navigate the labyrinth of life. Yet, at times, this wisdom can be overshadowed by the very limitations of aging—physical decline, forgetfulness, and an inability to adapt to the rapid changes of the world around them. In our culture's veneration of the elderly, we often overlook this complexity, falling into the assumption that age equals wisdom. But in doing so, we risk missing a deeper truth: that wisdom is a dynamic force, not a static one. It evolves, it challenges, and it requires active participation in life—not simply an accumulation of years. Wisdom is the willingness to question, to engage with life's uncertainties, to remain open to growth, no matter how old we become. In the end, the elder stands at the center of this paradox. They are both the product of time and the keeper of time's lessons. They offer us a vision of wisdom that is not just about the passage of years, but about the way we choose to live those years. And as we reflect on the elder's wisdom, we are reminded that age may grant us years, but it is what we do with those years that shapes the depth of our understanding. The paradox is not that wisdom is tied to age—but that it is never as simple as time alone. It is the interplay between life lived and life understood, between the accumulation of experiences and the capacity to learn from them, that creates wisdom's true value.

The idea of wisdom, as something shaped by experience, has deep roots in many philosophical traditions, each offering a unique lens through which to understand the relationship between life lived and knowledge gained. Whether framed through the reflective meditations of the Greek philosophers, the spiritual teachings of Eastern thought, or the modern perspectives that emphasize individualism and self-discovery, wisdom remains a central, yet ever-evolving, concept.

Greek Philosophy: Wisdom as Knowledge and Virtue

In ancient Greece, wisdom was not merely about the accumulation of knowledge, but the deep understanding of the *right* way to live. For the Greeks, wisdom was intricately tied to the ideal of virtue and the cultivation of one's character. Socrates famously claimed, *"The only true wisdom is in knowing you know nothing."* For Socrates, wisdom was not an intellectual accumulation, but the recognition of one's own limitations, the humility to acknowledge ignorance, and the perpetual striving to understand oneself and the world. This knowledge, however, was deeply practical: the wise person did not just know abstract truths but lived them. Plato, in his dialogues, extended this understanding of wisdom to the idea of knowledge in the truest sense—knowledge of the Forms, or the ideal versions of things, transcending the imperfect world of appearances. The philosopher-king in *The Republic* is the embodiment of this wisdom: a ruler who governs not just with practical intelligence, but with a profound understanding of eternal truths, guiding the state according to the highest ideals. For Plato, wisdom was not simply experiential knowledge, but the ability to perceive the deeper, immutable truths behind the fleeting world of senses. Aristotle, Plato's student, viewed wisdom somewhat differently. He believed that wisdom, or *sophia*, was the highest form of knowledge, achieved not just through theoretical understanding but through practical experience. Aristotle's concept of *phronesis*—practical wisdom—emphasized the importance of lived experience in understanding how to act rightly in the world. For him, wisdom was inseparable from experience; it was not something that could be taught purely through intellectual means but had to be cultivated through active engagement in the world, a gradual refinement of judgment shaped by repeated action and reflection.

Eastern Philosophy: Wisdom as Harmony and Inner Peace

In Eastern traditions, wisdom is often seen not as intellectual knowledge but as an experiential understanding that transcends the mind's dualities and cultivates harmony with the world. Whether in the teachings of Confucianism, Buddhism, or Taoism, wisdom is deeply tied to the cultivation of inner peace, ethical living, and an intimate relationship with the flow of life. In Confucian philosophy, wisdom (*zhi*) is one of the cardinal virtues, but it is inseparable from moral action and social harmony. Confucius emphasized the importance of learning through experience, particularly through the practice of ritual, self-discipline, and the cultivation of virtue within one's family and society. Wisdom, in the Confucian sense, was not a matter of theoretical knowledge but of moral discernment honed through constant practice. To be wise, one had to understand the natural order of things (*li*) and live in accordance with it—an understanding gained not from intellectual study alone but from the cultivation of good habits, relationships, and self-restraint. Similarly, in Buddhism, wisdom (*prajna*) is not merely knowledge, but a deep understanding of the nature of suffering, impermanence, and the interconnectedness of all things. Wisdom, in the Buddhist sense, is something that comes through personal experience—through meditation, mindfulness, and direct engagement with the nature of reality. It is a kind of experiential knowledge that transcends the ego, allowing one to see beyond the illusions of the self and experience the world as it truly is. Wisdom is often depicted as the culmination of a long process of self-purification, a gradual unraveling of ignorance and attachment, achieved only through direct personal experience rather than theoretical study. In this way, wisdom is as much about internal transformation as it is about external knowledge. In Taoism, wisdom is embodied in the concept of *wu wei*—the art of non-action or effortless action, where one aligns with the natural flow of the Tao (the Way). This wisdom is not derived from intellectual understanding but from living in harmony with nature, understanding the subtle rhythms of the world, and allowing life to unfold with ease. The Taoist sage embodies wisdom through simplicity, spontaneity, and balance, all qualities that are cultivated through intimate experience with the world, rather than through analysis or argument.

Modern Philosophy: Wisdom as Self-Realization and Practical Understanding

In modern philosophy, wisdom has evolved into a more individualistic, experiential concept. It is no longer confined to virtue or divine knowledge, but seen as an integral part of personal growth, self-realization, and practical understanding of life's challenges. Thinkers like Friedrich Nietzsche and Jean-Paul Sartre have redefined wisdom not as something transcendent or universally fixed, but as something deeply personal, bound to individual experience and freedom. Nietzsche, in particular, questioned the very notion of universal wisdom, arguing that traditional views of wisdom often stifled individual creativity and self-overcoming. For Nietzsche, wisdom was about embracing the challenges of life, confronting suffering, and learning to live authentically, free from societal conventions. Wisdom, in his eyes, was not a passive acceptance of the status quo but the active creation of one's own values and meaning. It was about living with courage in the face of life's uncertainties and embracing the fullness of experience, including hardship and suffering, as necessary components of self-creation. In existentialism, wisdom is also seen as a personal and transformative process. Sartre's concept of *authenticity* calls for the individual to confront the absurdity of life, to embrace freedom, and to take full responsibility for one's actions. Wisdom, from this perspective, arises from the recognition of one's freedom and the courage to face life's meaninglessness without resorting to false comforts. Experience, for existential thinkers, is not just a source of knowledge but a means of actively shaping one's identity and values.

In more contemporary views of wisdom, influenced by psychological and cognitive theories, wisdom is often seen as a form of practical judgment—the ability to navigate complex life situations with balance, perspective, and emotional regulation. Modern psychologists like Erik Erikson and Daniel Goleman have suggested that wisdom arises from the integration of cognitive maturity and emotional intelligence, with experience shaping the way we approach conflict, relationships, and the challenges of aging. Wisdom, in this view, is not just theoretical knowledge but an ability to apply one's experiences to make decisions that reflect a balanced, compassionate, and reflective approach to life.

Across all these traditions—whether ancient Greek philosophy, Eastern spiritual teachings, or modern psychological theory—wisdom emerges not as a static collection of facts, but as something deeply tied to lived experience. It is both shaped by the passage of time and actively cultivated through reflection, practice, and a willingness to engage with life's uncertainties. For the elder, wisdom is not a passive inheritance of years, but a product of a life well-lived, one in which experience, action, and reflection have come together to form something more than mere knowledge: an understanding of the world and oneself that transcends the fleeting and touches something timeless.

If wisdom is indeed a product of experience, the question arises: Does aging *automatically* grant wisdom, or does the passage of time risk turning experience into mere accumulation? The paradox of aging and wisdom lies in this tension: while age provides a framework for wisdom to emerge, it does not guarantee it. Time can shape the mind and the soul in two very different directions. For some, the accumulation of years fosters depth, insight, and clarity. For others, the same years, instead of sharpening perception, merely dull the senses and imprison the self in fixed patterns of thought. In one sense, it seems logical that the more time one spends navigating the complexities of life, the more likely they are to acquire wisdom. After all, the older we become, the more experiences we accumulate— encounters with joy, suffering, triumph, and loss—all of which hold lessons. Time can be the ultimate teacher, gently guiding us to a greater understanding of ourselves and the world. We witness others' mistakes, feel the weight of our own, and in time, we learn to approach life's challenges with more compassion, patience, and perspective. But the question remains: does time always *teach*? What of those who, with the passing years, seem increasingly resistant to change, locked in their ways and unwilling to grow? Here lies the flip side of the aging process: instead of wisdom, aging can sometimes lead to stagnation. For some, the accumulated years bring a hardening of the mind, a solidifying of views, and a narrowing of vision. As the years stack up, the world becomes less malleable; the elder's world may shrink to the familiar, the comfortable, the tried-and-true. The very essence of wisdom—openness to learning, adaptability, humility—can, over time, be suffocated by routine and certainty.

Aging, in this way, can become a process of retreat rather than growth. The mind, like the body, may lose its flexibility. The elder who ceases to question, to reconsider, or to challenge themselves risks becoming a prisoner of the past, clinging to outdated ideas and resisting the flow of change. It's in this way that wisdom can become a paradox. What should be the refinement of understanding may instead turn into the stagnation of knowledge. The elder's experiences, rather than leading to greater insight, become the shackles that bind them to a worldview that no longer serves them or their community. Perhaps the greatest risk in aging is not physical decline but mental atrophy—the slow erosion of the curiosity and openness that often define the wise. This is where the danger of *senility* comes in. In its most severe form, senility is not just the decline of memory but the fading of engagement with the world itself. A mind once rich with the fruits of experience can, in time, become dulled, disinterested, and even detached from the present moment. In this light, aging can seem like an existential trap: the more we live, the more likely we are to lose touch with the very things that gave life its meaning. Yet, this is not an inevitable fate. It is important to recognize that wisdom is not just a passive result of time's passing; it is also an active process. It is cultivated through ongoing reflection, a willingness to adapt, and the capacity to remain curious about the world. The paradox of aging and wisdom, then, is not that wisdom always comes with age, but that it requires a certain kind of engagement with life—an openness to transformation, a commitment to learning, and a refusal to let time harden the heart or freeze the mind. What differentiates those who age into wisdom from those who age into stagnation is, in part, their ability to continue asking questions, to see the world through new lenses, and to remain open to the possibility that the next chapter of their lives may hold new insights and challenges. It is in this *active* engagement with life's questions—rather than the passive accumulation of years—that wisdom flourishes. The elder who remains engaged, reflective, and inquisitive has the potential to offer the world not just the depth of their experiences, but the vitality of their continued growth. The danger lies in assuming that wisdom is simply a byproduct of time, that with enough years, it will emerge like a fine wine, automatically richer and more refined. In truth, wisdom demands attention and intention. It is not the automatic result of aging, but the thoughtful integration of experience, the continuous process of learning, and the courage to face life's complexities with an open heart and mind. Thus, the paradox remains. Aging can grant wisdom, but it can also lead to stagnation. The choice, in a way, is ours. It is the elder who actively embraces the challenges of the present, who remains willing to question and reflect, who stands the greatest chance of becoming the true guardian of wisdom, even as time continues its inexorable march forward. Aging, then, is not just a matter of how many years one has lived, but of how deeply one has lived those years. It is the engagement with life that transforms mere experience into wisdom.

If wisdom is not automatically granted by age, and if time itself can lead to stagnation or transformation, then the role of the elder as a guide becomes more complex. Throughout history, elders have been viewed as sources of wisdom—figures who, through the passage of years, have distilled the essence of life's truths and are entrusted with the task of imparting that knowledge to younger generations. But is the wisdom of the elderly truly a genuine truth, or is it, in part, a construct of societal expectations, a role assigned to them because of their age, experience, and position in the social hierarchy? This tension between genuine wisdom and societal expectations lies at the heart of how we view the elder. On one hand, there is a sense that wisdom, when cultivated through experience and reflection, is an objective and universal good. The elder, having lived through times of both prosperity and hardship, is assumed to possess an insight that transcends the limitations of the present. Their guidance is often seen as anchored in deep, hard-earned truth—a reflection of lessons learned over a lifetime. They have witnessed the cyclical nature of history, survived personal tragedies, and navigated the ebb and flow of human relationships. In this light, their wisdom feels almost timeless, a repository of knowledge that offers stability in a world constantly in flux. Yet, beneath this veneration of the elder's role as a guide, there lurks a subtle question: How much of the wisdom we attribute to the elder is shaped not by the elder's own experiences or insights, but by our expectations of them? The elder's role, after all, is not only a result of their lived experience but of the cultural norms that place them in positions of authority, respect, and reverence. In many societies, there is an unspoken agreement that age carries with it a certain kind of wisdom. But does age, by itself, confer the right to be a guide, or does society simply expect elders to fulfill this role, regardless of the quality of their insights? In some ways, the wisdom of the elder can be a social construct—a role that society projects onto those who have lived the longest, regardless of whether they have actively cultivated wisdom over the years. We expect the elder to be wise because that is the role they are supposed to play, and in turn, we may begin to see their guidance as a reflection of something universal, something inherently true, even when it is merely a reflection of cultural or familial norms. In this sense, wisdom becomes a kind of performance: the elder plays the role of the wise elder, and we, as society, invest that role with significance. But the problem with this view is clear. It places too much emphasis on societal expectations rather than on the actual depth of the elder's wisdom. The elder who fulfills the expectations of their role, but who has not spent their years cultivating critical thinking, reflection, or a deeper understanding of life's complexities, may still be seen as a figure of authority. Their wisdom may be more rooted in tradition, folklore, or inherited ways of thinking than in genuine, lived experience. It is easy for society to slip into the assumption that the elder's words are inherently profound, that their insights are rooted in truths that have been validated by the passage of time, even when those insights may be nothing more than the perpetuation of outdated beliefs or norms. This doesn't mean that the wisdom of elders is always false or shallow. On the contrary, many elders possess an extraordinary depth of understanding—born not just from experience but from an active engagement with life's mysteries. The elder who has embraced life's challenges, reflected on their experiences, and sought to understand the world in a deeper way can offer insights that go beyond cultural conditioning and into the realm of universal truth. The elder's wisdom, in this case, is not just a product of their age but a result of the conscious choices they have made to grow, to learn, and to engage with life. It is a wisdom earned through attention, reflection, and an openness to transformation, a wisdom that speaks not just to the past, but to the future. However, even the most genuinely wise elder is still part of a larger social and cultural framework that shapes how their wisdom is perceived and received. The very role of the elder as a guide is often steeped in expectation, influenced by the traditions and structures of the community in which they live. The respect accorded to elders can sometimes obscure the fact that wisdom, in its most genuine form, is not a static inheritance passed down through the generations, but a living, evolving process. Wisdom is not simply given; it must be earned, and the elder who remains passive in the face of change or who refuses to critically examine their own beliefs can, ironically, become less of a guide and more of an echo of the past. The role of the elder, then, is caught between two forces: the genuine potential for wisdom that comes with experience, and the expectations placed upon them by society. The elder is asked to be a guide, a source of wisdom, but must also contend with the weight of that expectation, which may sometimes obscure their ability to offer true, reflective insight. In this sense, the wisdom of the elder is not a singular, fixed thing but is subject to the context in which it is given and the qualities of the elder who gives it. Ultimately, the question of whether the elder's wisdom is genuine or merely a construct of societal expectations may not have a clear-cut answer.

It depends on the elder themselves, on how they choose to navigate the complexities of life and how they engage with the world around them. Wisdom, as always, is not a simple matter of age, but of reflection, growth, and a willingness to evolve. The elder who truly offers guidance does so not because of their years alone, but because they have taken the time to cultivate wisdom through an active, engaged life. In this way, the wisdom of the elder can be both a gift and a challenge—both a product of experience and a reflection of the ever-shifting expectations of the society in which they live.

In many cultures, the elder is seen as the guardian of tradition—the keeper of values, practices, and knowledge that have been passed down through the generations. This role positions the elder as a stabilizing force within society, a living connection to the past, the embodiment of collective memory. The wisdom of the elder, in this context, is often associated with the preservation of cultural, moral, and historical traditions. These traditions, deeply embedded in the social fabric, serve as guides for how to live, how to relate to others, and how to understand the world. The elder, as custodian, is tasked with transmitting these truths to the younger generation, ensuring that the lessons of the past endure and continue to shape the present and future. Yet, the role of the elder as a keeper of tradition is not without its tensions. The very traditions they seek to preserve are not static; they are living, breathing systems of meaning that must, at times, adapt to the changing needs and values of society. Here lies a delicate balancing act: how does the elder navigate the tension between honoring the past and recognizing the necessity of change and progress? How does one preserve the integrity of tradition while remaining open to new ideas, perspectives, and realities? It is this struggle that gives rise to one of the most enduring paradoxes of the elder's role: while they are venerated for their wisdom and connection to the past, they may also find themselves caught in the pull of an evolving world that demands change.

The elder as custodian of tradition often finds themselves as a bridge between generations, one foot firmly rooted in the history of the community and the other reaching towards the future. They are tasked with passing down customs and values, but these customs are not always unchanging. Societies evolve, and what was once a valuable tradition may no longer align with the realities or values of contemporary life. The elder, in this sense, faces a dilemma: how to maintain the integrity of the past without stifling the possibility of future growth. In some cases, the elder's wisdom may lie not just in preserving traditions but in knowing when to let go of them, or to transform them, in response to the shifting tides of culture. But this is not always easy. The pressure to preserve the old ways, to resist change, can be strong. Elders may find themselves reluctant to embrace new ideas, fearing that the erosion of tradition is an erosion of identity and moral order. In this view, tradition represents stability, continuity, and a source of meaning in an increasingly chaotic world. The elder, as a figure who has witnessed the passing of time, often sees themselves as a guardian of a truth that must not be lost. In their eyes, the new generation, with its penchant for novelty and innovation, may seem too quick to discard the wisdom of the past, too eager to reinvent the wheel without understanding the lessons that came before. This conflict between preserving tradition and embracing change is a central theme in Friedrich Nietzsche's critique of culture and tradition. Nietzsche, ever the critic of conventional values, saw tradition not as a source of wisdom, but as a force that constrained human potential. In his view, the elder— especially the elder entrenched in cultural and moral traditions—became a conservative force, clinging to old ideas that stifled growth and creativity. Nietzsche famously argued for the *Übermensch* (the "overman"), an individual who transcends the values and limitations imposed by tradition, creating their own path and meaning in life. From this perspective, the elder who is too attached to the past is a hindrance to human flourishing, a figure who holds society back from its true potential by insisting on the relevance of outdated norms and beliefs. For Nietzsche, tradition is often a form of oppression, a constraint that limits human potential by binding people to the past rather than encouraging them to confront the future with fresh eyes and a new vision. The elder, as the custodian of these traditions, can therefore be seen as both a source of wisdom and an obstacle to progress. If wisdom is simply the repetition of what has always been, then it risks becoming stagnant, preventing the individual from engaging with the world in a way that is truly transformative. The elder's attachment to the past, in this view, is not wisdom but a form of nostalgia—a desire to preserve what is familiar at the cost of growth, change, and innovation. But is tradition inherently oppressive? Can the elder's role as custodian of tradition truly limit human potential, or does it provide a necessary anchor in a world increasingly adrift? To say that tradition is always oppressive would be an oversimplification. In many cases, traditions are not only important for cultural continuity but also for personal and collective identity. They provide a sense of belonging, a moral compass, and a framework for understanding the world. The elder, as the bearer of these traditions, is not necessarily holding society back, but rather helping to maintain the wisdom that has accumulated over generations. They pass on stories, rituals, and values that have guided their communities through both triumph and hardship. These traditions, in this light, are not shackles but the very foundation upon which societies build and evolve. Moreover, the elder as custodian of tradition is not simply a passive figure who enforces the status quo. Many elders, through their life experience, develop a nuanced understanding of when and how tradition should evolve. They understand that traditions are not immutable; they are living practices that can adapt to new circumstances. The truly wise elder is one who recognizes that while the past has much to offer, the future requires innovation. The elder, in this sense, is not just a keeper of the old ways, but a mediator between past and future, holding the tension between preservation and transformation. Ultimately, the question of whether tradition is a form of wisdom or a form of oppression depends on how it is applied and understood. Tradition, when rooted in living wisdom and flexible to change, can be a source of deep meaning and connection. But when it becomes a rigid structure that refuses to evolve, it can indeed become a force that limits human potential. The elder, in their role as custodian, must constantly navigate this tension—between honoring the past and embracing the future, between preserving what is valuable and letting go of what no longer serves. It is in this balance that the elder's true wisdom lies, for the true custodian of tradition knows that the wisdom of the past must always be tempered with the vitality of the present and the promise of the future.

The role of the elder as a figure of wisdom is undeniably intertwined with the notion of authority. In many societies, elders are not just repositories of knowledge but also moral leaders—individuals whose judgments and guidance are seen as critical in maintaining the ethical fabric of their communities. But this raises a significant ethical question: Are elders moral leaders in their own right, or do they simply occupy a position of authority by virtue of their age? Furthermore, how do the dynamics of power between the elder and the younger generations influence not only the flow of wisdom but also the moral decisions that shape society?

Authority, as it is traditionally understood, is often linked to power—the ability to influence, command, and guide. In the case of the elderly, this authority is often seen as *natural*, a byproduct of their years, experiences, and the social structures that elevate age to a position of respect. But the ethics of aging demand that we question whether authority granted by age alone is morally justified. Does the mere passage of time confer wisdom and moral insight, or is it the elder's actions, character, and personal development over the years that truly establish their right to guide others?

The dynamics of power between elders and younger generations are critical to understanding this question. In traditional societies, the elder's authority often goes unchallenged, resting on a presumption that age equals wisdom and moral clarity. Young people are expected to respect, defer to, and follow the guidance of elders—be they parents, community leaders, or spiritual authorities. The older generation's power, then, is deeply embedded in the structure of the community, where the knowledge of the past is viewed as invaluable to the stability and continuation of cultural and moral norms. This vertical relationship, however, can sometimes foster an imbalance, where the younger generation feels obligated to follow the elder's lead without questioning the foundations of that authority. Here, power is wielded not just in guiding behavior but in shaping beliefs and ideals—sometimes without regard for whether these beliefs remain relevant or morally sound in the face of changing times.

However, this unquestioned reverence for age can also be problematic. The mere fact of aging does not necessarily confer moral clarity. Wisdom is not automatically achieved by the accumulation of years; it is, in many ways, a result of an ongoing, active engagement with life's moral and intellectual challenges. Age without self-reflection, without the willingness to adapt to new ethical considerations or to reevaluate outdated beliefs, risks becoming a source of stagnation rather than growth. The authority of the elder, if untempered by wisdom and personal development, may become less a force for good and more a means of perpetuating dogma, reinforcing outdated ideas, or stifling innovation and moral progress. This brings us to the philosophical concept of *natural authority*. Traditionally, the elder's authority has been seen as an organic extension of their age—a kind of inherent moral legitimacy. After all, the longer one lives, the more they experience, and thus, the more likely they are to develop a nuanced understanding of the world. But is this assumption of authority truly justified? Is the moral wisdom that is often ascribed to the elder simply a result of their time on earth, or does it require intentional growth and self-examination? Consider the idea that authority, particularly moral authority, should not be automatic. Instead, it should be earned through the cultivation of virtue, the openness to learning, and the capacity to evolve one's views in response to new ideas and experiences. The elder who simply "has lived through it" may have a wealth of personal experiences, but this does not necessarily translate into moral insight or wisdom. The true moral leader is one who, through the years, has developed not only knowledge but also self-awareness, compassion, and a commitment to ethical living. It is the elder who has intentionally sought to cultivate wisdom, who has worked to understand the deeper questions of life, who becomes a source of genuine moral authority—not because of their age alone but because of their capacity for reflection and growth. This leads us to the complex relationship between wisdom and authority. The elder, ideally, should be both a figure of wisdom and a figure of authority, and it is in the duality of these roles that their influence on moral decision-making becomes most profound. The elder as a figure of wisdom brings to bear not only knowledge but perspective, understanding, and insight—qualities that are essential for guiding moral choices. Wisdom allows the elder to navigate the complexities of human nature and societal needs with a deeper sense of empathy and fairness. Authority, on the other hand, provides the elder with the power to enact that wisdom in a way that can affect real change, shaping the moral landscape of their community. But how does this duality affect the moral decision-making of society at large? When an elder occupies both positions—both as a wellspring of knowledge and as an authoritative figure—their influence extends beyond personal guidance. They shape the very ethical framework within which society operates, often determining what is considered "right" and "wrong," what is valued and what is not. This dual role, however, is not without its challenges. When wisdom and authority are aligned, they can guide a society toward ethical growth and moral clarity. But when authority becomes divorced from wisdom—when age becomes the sole measure of legitimacy—there is a risk that moral decision-making becomes rigid, outdated, and out of step with the needs of the present. In this sense, the elder's authority, though rooted in tradition, must be continually questioned and reassessed. Moral leadership is not a one-time inheritance but an ongoing responsibility. To be a moral leader, the elder must not only offer wisdom but also be willing to examine their own biases, adapt to the changing moral landscape, and be receptive to the critiques and insights of younger generations. The power of the elder must not be wielded as a tool of control but as a means of fostering moral growth and evolution within society. Thus, the ethics of aging and authority are complex, as they encompass both the wisdom that comes with experience and the power that is often assumed with age. The elder's role is not simply to maintain the moral status quo but to engage in an active dialogue with the generations that follow, guiding them not by blind authority, but through thoughtful leadership. Wisdom and authority, when in harmony, have the potential to lead society toward a deeper understanding of ethics and morality—one that is not bound by the past, but one that continues to evolve, reflect, and adapt as it moves into the future.

As the elder stands at the threshold of the final chapters of life, they become not just a figure of wisdom or authority, but a poignant symbol of mortality itself. Aging, in its most fundamental way, confronts us with our finite nature, an inevitable reminder that all things—human lives included—are transient. In this confrontation with time's inexorable march, the elder embodies the paradox of human existence: they are living witnesses to both the impermanence of life and the possibility of meaning in the face of it. To encounter the elderly is, in many ways, to come face to face with death itself—not in the literal sense of their passing, but in the existential weight they carry, as living symbols of the decay and eventual end that awaits us all. In this light, the elder's very existence becomes a complex meditation on mortality. Their aging body, frail and weathered, speaks volumes about the passage of time—the irreversible processes of decay that govern all life. Yet, in this decay, there is also a deep and profound truth: the elder stands as a reminder that, in the face of inevitable death, there is still meaning to be found. The elder's life, filled with years of accumulated experience, stands as proof that, even as bodies age and fade, there remains the possibility of richness, wisdom, and purpose. The elder is not merely a figure of loss, but also one of enduring meaning, for in the awareness of mortality, there lies the potential for a deeper engagement with life's fundamental questions. The concept of mortality has been central to existential philosophy, and among the thinkers who have engaged with this notion in profound ways is Martin Heidegger. In his exploration of human existence, Heidegger famously introduced the idea of *Being-toward-death*, a fundamental aspect of what it means to be human. For Heidegger, our awareness of our mortality shapes our very being. It is not just the inevitability of death, but the awareness of that inevitability, that defines us as human beings. We are, in essence, creatures who live in anticipation of death, and it is in this awareness that we find the potential for meaning and authenticity in our lives.

The elder, in their advanced years, becomes a living testament to Heidegger's *Being-toward-death*. They have come to terms, often consciously, with the finite nature of their own existence. For the elderly, time is no longer an abstract concept, but a daily reality—the future is no longer a distant horizon, but something that looms ever closer. The elder's relationship with death, therefore, is not theoretical; it is immediate, real, and tangible. And yet, this confrontation with death is not merely one of despair. Heidegger suggests that it is through our awareness of mortality that we come to live more authentically. The recognition that our time is limited forces us to engage more fully with life, to make choices that are meaningful and deliberate. For the elderly, this awareness of mortality may lead to a profound reevaluation of life's purpose. In the face of death, many elders turn inward, seeking to understand what their life has meant, what legacies they leave behind, and how they have shaped the world they inhabit. The question of meaning becomes more urgent as the years pass. What was the point of all the striving, the accumulation of knowledge, the creation of relationships, the pursuit of goals? In the final stages of life, the elder faces the ultimate existential question: What is the value of a life, once it is nearing its end? This confrontation with mortality forces the elder to grapple with the tension between the passage of time and the possibility of meaning, to make peace with the idea that life may not be everlasting, but that it can still be *meaningful*. This philosophical journey is not just a passive acceptance of mortality but an active quest for purpose in the twilight years. The elder, having lived through the major transitions and milestones of life, often experiences a deep, existential reckoning. The final stages of life are not just a countdown to death, but an opportunity for reflection, for distilling meaning from a life that has been lived. For some, this process may involve a deepening of spirituality, coming to terms with regrets, or an attempt to make amends with loved ones. For others, it may simply be a quiet acceptance, a letting go of the need for any definitive answers and embracing the mystery of existence as it is. Aging, then, is not merely a process of physical decline but a deeply philosophical journey—one that invites the elderly to explore the meaning of their existence in ways they may not have done earlier in life. It is the opportunity to reflect on the choices made, the paths not taken, and the relationships that have shaped their identity. The elder's life, in its final stages, becomes a canvas for existential reflection, an inquiry into the significance of what has been lived and what remains to be understood. It is, in a sense, a final invitation to confront death—not as a tragic end but as a defining feature of the human condition. The elder, as the face of mortality, reminds us that death is not something that lies waiting at the end of life, but something that shapes life itself. In acknowledging our mortality, we are given the chance to live more fully, more authentically, and more meaningfully. The elder's confrontation with death, then, is not merely a confrontation with loss, but with the very essence of what it means to be alive. They stand as proof that even in the face of the inevitable, life can still hold meaning, that wisdom can still be cultivated, and that the search for purpose never truly ends, even as the body fades and time runs out. Thus, the elder's experience of aging is not just a personal journey but a philosophical one—a profound exploration of what it means to be human, to confront death, and to find meaning in the face of impermanence. The elder, with all their accumulated years, becomes both a reminder of our mortality and a testament to the possibility of meaning within it. And it is in this delicate balance— between life's fleeting nature and the wisdom that can arise from facing it—that we find the deepest lessons about living authentically, in full awareness of both the finite and the eternal.

In the existential landscape, the tension between youth and age has long been a battleground for the forces of creativity, vitality, and tradition. Youth, with its boundless energy and hunger for new horizons, often stands in stark contrast to the elder, whose wisdom is rooted in the slow accumulation of years and the weight of tradition. The very essence of youth can seem like a rebellion against the stagnation of age—a dynamic, restless push toward self-assertion and self-expression that feels, at times, incompatible with the elder's measured, conservative approach to life. Is the energy of youth, then, a reaction against the stagnation of the elder? Or is it something deeper—an existential force seeking to break free from the constraints imposed by a past that seems increasingly irrelevant? Friedrich Nietzsche's critique of aging and tradition provides a powerful lens through which to view this tension. Nietzsche, who viewed life as a constant struggle for the *will to power*, saw the influence of elders and their reverence for tradition as a force that stifled individual creativity and personal growth. For Nietzsche, the elder, particularly one who is rooted in past norms and conventions, represents an obstacle to the flourishing of the individual, a figure whose authority is based not on the strength of their personal will but on the weight of social convention. The elder, in this view, becomes a symbol of *becoming stagnant*, a person whose wisdom is no longer an evolving force but a rigid system of inherited beliefs that stand in the way of progress. The vitality of youth, for Nietzsche, is precisely what has the power to overcome this stagnant force, to push the individual beyond the limiting boundaries of the past, and to carve a new path forward.

Youth, in this Nietzschean sense, is not merely an age of physical vitality but a manifestation of the will to overcome—an impulse that drives the individual toward self-creation and self-transcendence. It is the creative, experimental phase of life, in which the individual is free to challenge and reshape the world around them. In Nietzsche's philosophy, this energy is essential, for it is only by embracing the potential for constant self-overcoming that humanity can evolve, adapt, and achieve greatness. The elder, by contrast, represents the opposite impulse: the desire to preserve, to hold onto what has been, to avoid change in favor of continuity. In Nietzsche's world, this is a reactionary force, one that preserves the status quo at the expense of innovation, freedom, and creative expression. But while Nietzsche's philosophy often places youth in opposition to the elder, there is a deeper question: Can the vitality of youth ever truly overcome the wisdom of the elder? Or, conversely, must it learn from and integrate the elder's experience to fully realize its potential? This is where the tension between the impulse for self-overcoming and the reverence for inherited wisdom becomes most pronounced. On one hand, youth's thirst for originality and the desire to break free from established constraints can seem irreconcilable with the elder's emphasis on tradition, memory, and preservation. Youth, in this sense, is the force that seeks to transcend the past in favor of creating a new world—one that is not bound by the moral, cultural, or philosophical limitations that the elder holds dear. Yet, there is another perspective, one that sees the wisdom of the elder not as a limitation but as a necessary foundation for the vitality of youth. Without the knowledge passed down through the generations, the energy of youth risks becoming aimless, untethered, and potentially destructive. The desire to overcome and transcend must have a grounding in experience, for it is only through the wisdom of the past that youth can understand what is worth overcoming and what is simply an echo of youthful folly. In this way, youth's vitality can learn from the elder's wisdom—not in the sense of simply mimicking it, but by engaging with it critically, drawing from it the lessons and values that can help shape the future. This tension between the will to power and the reverence for tradition is most sharply embodied in Nietzsche's concept of the *Übermensch*—the "overman," or "superman," who transcends the limitations of both society and the past in order to create a new, more authentic existence. The

Übermensch is the ultimate individual, one who does not simply accept the values of the elder or the culture around them but creates their own path, their own meaning, and their own destiny. However, this figure of self-overcoming does not exist in a vacuum; it is always engaged with the forces of culture, history, and tradition. The *Übermensch* does not erase the past, but rather *transcends* it—integrating its lessons while surpassing its limitations. The vitality of youth, in Nietzsche's vision, is precisely what allows the individual to overcome the old ways, but this overcoming is not an act of destruction; it is one of creative transformation. In this sense, youth and the elderly are not necessarily in opposition but in dialogue. The vitality of youth pushes the boundaries of what is possible, but it does so in conversation with the wisdom of the elder. The elder offers not simply guidance, but a context—a framework within which youth can navigate the complexities of life. The challenge for youth, then, is not to reject the elder's wisdom wholesale, but to engage with it critically, to see it not as a constraint but as a resource from which to draw the energy and direction needed to create something new. Thus, the philosophical tension between the impulse for self-overcoming and the reverence for inherited wisdom is not one that can be easily resolved. The energy of youth cannot simply discard the wisdom of the elder; nor can the elder's wisdom be the sole guide for a life that must constantly evolve and adapt to new circumstances. In the end, it is in the synthesis of these forces—in the integration of vitality and wisdom—that the greatest potential for human growth lies. The youthful impulse to create, challenge, and innovate must learn to respect and draw from the deep well of experience and tradition that the elder represents. And the elder, in turn, must recognize that wisdom is not an end point, but a starting place—a foundation upon which the future can be built. Only through this dynamic interplay of energy and experience can humanity truly move forward, transcending the past while honoring its lessons, and creating a world that is both new and wise.

In a world that is increasingly defined by rapid technological advancements, constant innovation, and a relentless pursuit of progress, the figure of the elderly seems to be caught in a precarious balancing act. Once revered as the guardians of wisdom, cultural memory, and moral authority, elders now often find themselves marginalized in societies that value youth, novelty, and efficiency above all else. The elder, in this context, can appear almost anachronistic—a relic of a bygone era when time moved more slowly and tradition held greater sway. But is this the inevitable fate of the elderly in modernity, or can they still play a vital, transformative role in a world defined by constant change? The tension between the elder and the contemporary world is most apparent in the existential dilemma faced by aging individuals today. Modern society, with its obsession for speed, productivity, and innovation, has little room for the elder's slower, more reflective pace. Youth, with its boundless energy and focus on the future, is often seen as the driving force of progress, while the elder, whose life has unfolded in a more deliberate and measured way, is viewed as less relevant, or even burdensome. In a society that places such high value on productivity—where the question of "What have you done lately?" reigns supreme—the elder's place in the social fabric feels increasingly precarious. Their accumulated experience, once considered invaluable, now seems to be in competition with a culture that prizes innovation above all else. Yet, the existential question remains: can the elderly adapt to this fast-changing world? Can they contribute meaningfully to a society that seems so at odds with their more measured, experience-based approach to life? The answer is complex, for it hinges on how we understand the role of the elderly in modernity. If we view elders as mere relics of a past that no longer serves the present, then their relevance is surely diminished. But if we understand the elder's value not as a force for stagnation, but as a potential symbol of wisdom, resilience, and continuity, then their place in modern society becomes far more dynamic. In this sense, the elder has the potential to become more than just a figure of nostalgia. They can serve as the living embodiment of a deeper, more sustainable relationship with time—one that transcends the immediate demands of the present and embraces the long view of history, culture, and human nature. In a world that seems perpetually caught in the grip of the new and the now, the elder stands as a reminder that there is value in reflection, in understanding the patterns of the past, and in accepting the inevitable rhythms of life. Their wisdom is not just about the past, but about navigating the future with a sense of continuity and groundedness.

The existential dilemma for the elderly in modernity, then, is not just a personal crisis but a social one. In a world that prizes youth and productivity, what does it mean to age with dignity, to retain one's relevance, and to contribute meaningfully? The elder is forced to reckon with the tension between their own experience and the societal values that increasingly deem them irrelevant. The very notion of *being* an elder in a world so focused on the future often requires a reinvention—a reimagining of what it means to be wise, what it means to have authority, and how that authority can be shaped in a society that seems to have little use for it. In the realm of modern philosophy, this dilemma is being rethought. No longer is the elder figure necessarily confined to the role of conservative, passive guardian of tradition. Modern thinkers have begun to explore the possibility of the elderly as a symbol of wisdom and resilience in the face of an uncertain future. In the wake of climate change, political instability, and technological disruption, elders have the potential to offer something invaluable to society: the ability to *slow down*, to reflect, and to approach the future not as a race to be won, but as a journey to be understood. The elder's role, then, is not to resist change, but to *integrate* change into a larger, more thoughtful narrative about human life, values, and the world we are creating. Philosophers in the 21st century, such as Zygmunt Bauman and Alain de Botton, have called for a reconsideration of what it means to age in a world that prioritizes acceleration and novelty. In contrast to the technocratic imperative to optimize and maximize every moment, these thinkers urge us to slow down and reflect, to embrace the process of aging not as a decline, but as an opportunity for growth in its own right. The elder, when reimagined in this context, becomes not a relic of the past, but a beacon for the future—a figure who brings wisdom to bear on the challenges that lie ahead, and who can help guide society through periods of uncertainty, chaos, and transformation. The elder's potential to contribute meaningfully to modern society, then, lies in their ability to act as a counterbalance to the relentless pursuit of progress. Where modernity tends to focus on the *new*, the elder's wisdom reminds us of the value of the *old*. In a world that is often too focused on innovation, the elder offers the necessary reminder that not everything new is necessarily better, and that in the rush to advance, we may be losing sight of the values that ground us. Their role is not to resist change, but to ensure that change is anchored in something deeper, something enduring. Thus, in modernity, the elder's place is neither guaranteed nor easily defined, but it is far from obsolete. Rather than being relegated to the sidelines of society, the elder has the opportunity to become a key figure in navigating the complexities of contemporary life. They are not merely a symbol of a world that is passing away, but a potential force for resilience, reflection, and meaning in a world that is desperately searching for stability amidst constant flux. In a time of unprecedented change, the elderly have the unique opportunity to offer a steady hand—to remind us that in the face of uncertainty, wisdom is still a necessary and powerful force, and that the lessons of the past are never entirely irrelevant, even in the future we are still trying to build. In this reimagined role, the elder becomes not an anachronism but an ideal—an ideal of wisdom, endurance, and resilience in a world that is increasingly uncertain, increasingly fast, and increasingly hungry for something deeper. In the end, the figure of the elder emerges not merely as a marker of the passage of time, but as a profound symbol of reflection, self-overcoming, and transformation. The elder embodies a unique kind of wisdom—one that arises from the slow unfolding of life's complexities, its joys, and its sorrows. As they age, they are not simply witnesses to the world's changing tides, but active participants in an ongoing journey of philosophical introspection. In this sense, aging becomes not a process of decline, but one of continuous growth and redefinition. The elder, through their experience, shows us that wisdom does not come from mere accumulation, but from a reflective engagement with life itself, a willingness to question and revise one's beliefs, and an openness to both internal and external transformation. At the heart of this philosophical journey is the task of integrating wisdom and vitality. It is a delicate dance between honoring the lessons of the past and embracing the possibilities of the future. The elder is not bound by time, but instead learns to live with it—understanding both its limits and its potential. This is where a truly inclusive philosophy of aging must begin: by acknowledging the complexities of growing old, not as a process to be feared or avoided, but as an opportunity to deepen one's understanding of life, of meaning, and of death. In a culture obsessed with youth and productivity, aging too often becomes seen as a burden or an afterthought. Yet, as we have seen, the elder carries with them a treasure trove of insight that is not to be dismissed but celebrated. The elder's contribution to the broader philosophical project—this continuous search for meaning—is irreplaceable. In their quiet wisdom, in their measured steps through life, they offer a model of how to confront the fundamental questions of existence. They remind us that time is finite, that life is both fragile and resilient, and that in every moment, there is a potential for growth, for deeper understanding, and for the kind of transcendence that comes from fully embracing our humanity. Through the elder, we come to see that the philosophical journey is not a linear path but a series of layers, each providing its own revelations and challenges. The elderly, with their perspective earned through years of experience, offers us the invaluable lesson that aging, too, is an integral part of the search for meaning. Ultimately, the question remains: does the elder represent a model of a philosophical life lived in harmony with time, or is their life a reminder that every stage of existence is filled with both constraints and possibilities for transcendence? Perhaps the answer is both. The elder is not immune to the constraints imposed by time—bodily decay, the inevitable limitations of memory, the sense of a future that grows smaller with each passing year. Yet it is within these very constraints that the elder finds the opportunity for transcendence. For in acknowledging the fragility of life, in confronting death as an ever-present companion, the elder taps into a deeper well of wisdom, one that allows them to live with intention, with gratitude, and with a sense of peace that comes from fully embracing both the past and the future. Aging, in this light, is not merely about the decline of the body, but the flourishing of the soul. The elder teaches us that every stage of life, even as it brings its own set of limitations, offers the potential for transcendence. It is through the lens of aging that we begin to see life not as a race to be won, but as a journey to be understood—one that involves both self-overcoming and self-acceptance. The elder, in their quiet dignity, becomes the living proof that wisdom is not something to be gained and then held onto, but something that must continuously be lived, challenged, and renewed. In embracing the elderly, we are invited to reimagine aging not as an end, but as a beginning—a new phase of life in which reflection, wisdom, and vitality come together to create something profound and lasting. The elder is not simply a figure of the past, but a crucial player in the unfolding narrative of human existence, showing us that the journey toward understanding life, meaning, and death is never complete. It is ongoing, evolving, and always full of the possibility for transcendence, even in the final stages of life.

Chapter 7

The Due Fear

"He who has a why to live can bear almost any how."

~ Friedrich Nietzsche

Death, that final and absolute conclusion to the human struggle, is the one certainty that stands in defiance of all our delusions of control and power. We are born with the knowledge of its eventual arrival, yet we spend the majority of our lives as if it were a distant myth, a tale for old age or an abstraction for those unlucky enough to meet it prematurely. How fragile, how absurd is our pretense! We dance, we fight, we conquer—thinking we outrun death with every passing moment. But death, in its inevitability, mocks our attempts to escape it. What is life, if not a series of fleeting triumphs, moments of chaos, and bursts of meaning, all fleeting before the dark horizon of non-being? It is easy to ignore the abyss. It is easy to think of death as something 'out there,' something that happens to others. But the abyss is not outside us; it is within us. We are born with the shadow of mortality cast upon our every action, and it is in recognizing this shadow that we might grasp the true nature of our existence. To live in full consciousness of death—this is not nihilism, but the truest form of freedom. For it is only in the face of our finitude that we come to understand what it means to live authentically. Only in knowing that we are *not* immortal, that we cannot delay our reckoning, do we come to grasp the urgency, the responsibility, and the power inherent in existence itself.

Why, then, do we fear death? Is it the specter of the unknown that haunts us—the anxiety of what lies beyond the veil of life? Or is it something more profound, a visceral terror rooted in our awareness of life's fragility and impermanence? To look upon death is to peer into the great abyss, and we fear what we cannot control, what we cannot predict, what we cannot grasp. Perhaps, at its core, our fear is not of death itself, but of what death reveals about us. The fact that life—our life—can end, abruptly, without warning, is the very thing we cannot bear to face. In our daily routines, we seek distractions, build walls of security, and bury ourselves in the illusion of immortality. Yet, death remains a mirror, showing us that everything we have, everything we are, is fleeting. It is a reminder that the moment we experience—this breath, this heartbeat, this fleeting spark of awareness—will one day be gone. The fear of death may then be the fear of facing our own transience. The fear that what we have fought for, what we have strived to build, will dissolve into dust, that all of our triumphs and suffering will be erased in the face of a single, inevitable end. This realization— far from being a denial of meaning—can be the very thing that gives life its sharpest edge. Death teaches us that we are not eternal, that time is the most precious of commodities, and that the fleeting nature of life is what imbues it with urgency and meaning. In fearing death, we are not merely fearing what comes after, but what we must lose to arrive at that final moment. We are afraid because we do not know how to reconcile the beauty of life with its inherent fragility. But perhaps it is only through facing death head-on, through embracing its inevitability, that we can learn how to live with greater clarity, purpose, and courage. For it is only in acknowledging our finitude that we can begin to live with the fullness and intensity that the moment demands.

I've had moments in my life that were shaped by the stark presence of death, moments that, at the time, felt like they were part of something far larger and more incomprehensible than I could understand. One such moment occurred when I was a child, a time when the world felt endlessly wide and full of possibility, and death was just an abstract concept—something that happened in stories or to other people. But that day, in the front passenger seat of my father's car, it felt as though I brushed against it with startling clarity.

We were on our way to the hospital, where I often spent my holidays playing around my father's office and passing time with him. As we neared the hospital, my impatience surged. I opened the car door, thinking I'd be the first one out, eager to run ahead, as children are. But the door swung open faster than I anticipated, and before I could even realize it, I was thrown out of the moving car, tumbling onto the road, rolling uncontrollably. In that split second, as the world flipped and spun around me, I saw the wheels of an oncoming bus hurtling toward me. Everything seemed to slow down in that moment—time stretched as I lay helpless, exposed on the tarmac. The bus, coming toward me at speed, had no way of avoiding me. But the driver reacted just in time. It was then that I understood, for the first time, how fragile life was. Had the bus not stopped in time, it would have been my last day.

That experience remained with me, a visceral reminder that death can arrive unexpectedly, when we least expect it, even in the moments we think we are safest. It's easy to believe we are invincible when we are young, but in the blink of an eye, everything can change. My father, a man whose life had been marked by loss and violence, would often tell me stories of his own confrontations with death—stories of conflict and tragedy that seemed to shadow his every step. He would recount the days when he and his uncles lived in constant danger, caught in a conflict that lasted for over two decades. His father, my grandfather, was a police officer who had been shot and killed while returning home from his duties, a casualty of a violent world that didn't care for the quiet moments of life. My father's voice would grow quiet when he spoke of those years—the deaths he had seen, the constant threat of violence that hung over them all. Death was something he had known intimately, not as an abstract fear, but as a relentless companion, one that had stolen many from his life. These stories, often shared in passing, shaped my understanding of mortality. I could not help but see that in both my near-death experience and my father's recounting of loss, death was not just a distant, inevitable truth. It was immediate, something that could enter our lives at any moment, without warning or mercy. In that way, death became less of a fear and more of a lesson, one that taught me about the fragility of our existence. For my father, who had survived so much, there was a kind of quiet wisdom in his acceptance of death—he knew it was not something we could avoid or control, but something that could shape how we lived. Perhaps, in facing it so often, he had come to live with a sense of urgency, appreciating the fleeting moments between birth and death, and valuing what was most important: family, connection, and the simple acts of living. For me, that day on the road was more than just a close call. It was a confrontation with mortality that, though I didn't fully comprehend it at the time, would stay with me, shaping how I thought about the preciousness of life. It taught me to be present, to not take time for granted, and to understand that death, while inevitable, does not diminish the value of the life we have—it heightens it, giving it a depth and clarity that might otherwise be lost in the rush of our daily routines. The truth is, death does not arrive on our terms. It can take us when we are unprepared, or it can haunt us in the stories of others—those who have faced it, and those who have seen it come too soon. But in confronting it, whether through loss, near-miss, or reflection, we are offered the chance to live more fully, more consciously, aware of the fragility of each moment.

Maaz was a classmate who sat beside me during school hours. He once shared with me that he preferred dying before his parents, a statement that revealed a deeper fear – not just of death, but of the pain of witnessing the death of loved ones.

I still recall the conversation vividly, though the context surrounding it has faded with time. Maaz turned to me and said, "I'd prefer dying before my parents. I can't imagine a world without them, and they're strong enough to cope with my loss." In that moment, I realized that Maaz's fear wasn't just about his own mortality; it was about the emotional pain of losing those who mattered most. His words verbalized a fear I hadn't dared to acknowledge – the fear of living in a world without my parents. Maaz's desire to die before his parents wasn't about escaping death; it was about avoiding the unbearable pain of witnessing their passing. Maaz's story is a poignant reminder that the fear of death is often intertwined with the fear of loss. His unusual desire may seem counterintuitive, but it reveals a deeper psychological complexity – a complexity that many of us can relate to. As I reflect on our conversation, I realize that Maaz's silent tragedy is one that many of us face, often in silence and solitude.

The fear of others' mortality often intertwines with our own existential anxieties, forming a mirror in which we see the fragility of our being. When we grieve for others, are we truly mourning their departure, or are we recoiling from the stark reminder that we, too, are finite? The thought of death—raw, unyielding, and inevitable—forces us to confront questions we often suppress: What does it mean to exist? What remains when we cease? It is tempting to argue that the fear of mortality stems from the unknown—a void we cannot comprehend. But perhaps it is not the mystery of death itself that terrifies us. Instead, it is the emotional wreckage left in its wake: the pain of absence, the dissolution of connections, the abrupt ending of shared stories. Death unravels the fabric of relationships, and in doing so, it forces us to acknowledge how tethered we are to others for meaning and identity. Yet there's more. The death of someone close can feel like a rupture in the continuity of life, exposing us to the precariousness of our own existence. We see in their passing not only the loss of what they brought to our world but also a reflection of what awaits us—a cessation of roles, relationships, and the narratives we craft to shield ourselves from impermanence. Fear of mortality is not singular; it is layered. On one level, it speaks to a deeply personal dread of ceasing to be. On another, it encapsulates the sorrow of living in a world where love and loss are inseparable. In this duality, perhaps, lies the crux of our terror. We fear death not solely for the void it creates within us, but for the realization that life, in its fleeting beauty, is defined by what—and who—we must eventually leave behind. The philosophical challenge, then, is not to conquer the fear of mortality but to reconcile with it. To see death not as an intruder upon life but as its inevitable counterpart—a force that, in its shadow, compels us to live more vividly, to connect more deeply, and to cherish what we cannot keep. Only by embracing the impermanence of existence can we hope to find solace in the transient yet profound connections that make life meaningful.

If the fear of death compels us to confront our own impermanence, grief drags us into the heart of love's paradox: the deeper our attachments, the more we open ourselves to loss. Love, in its essence, binds us to others, weaving connections so profound that they seem to transcend time. Yet, it is precisely these bonds that render us vulnerable to grief, the aching void left when those connections are severed by mortality.

Grief is not merely sorrow; it is the reverberation of love meeting its limit. When someone we care for dies, we don't just mourn their absence—we grieve the silencing of shared moments, the unfulfilled potential of what could have been. The laughter that no longer fills the room, the warmth of presence now turned to memory, are reminders of life's impermanence and the unrelenting passage of time. This complex relationship between love and loss underpins the existential dread we feel toward grief. My mother told me that our grandmother was the last of her siblings and saw each of them pass away before her. At their deaths, she would quietly say, "Please, death, be gentle on my siblings; they are the last remnants of my mother's children." Her words echoed a profound understanding of mortality, not as an abstract concept, but as a lived reality intertwined with love and loss. In her plea, there was an acceptance of death's inevitability, coupled with a tender wish for compassion in its approach. To love deeply is to tether a piece of ourselves to another, making their departure feel like a fracturing of our own being. Attachment amplifies this vulnerability, for the more entwined our lives become with others, the greater the weight of their absence. Yet grief, as agonizing as it is, serves as an affirmation of life's depth and intensity. It testifies to the power of connection, revealing that the pain of loss is inseparable from the joy of love. Without attachment, there is no grief; without grief, we cannot grasp the magnitude of what we have cherished. Perhaps, then, the challenge is to navigate this fragile duality—to love fully despite the inevitability of loss, to find meaning in the fleeting, and to accept that the pain of grief is not an adversary but a reflection of life's richest moments. It is in this delicate balance that we confront our fear of others' mortality, recognizing that while love binds us to the temporal, it also grants us a glimpse of the eternal through its enduring impact on our hearts.

Sir Khattak, a successful author, a teacher in his seventies—an age that mirrored the wisdom and authority of a father figure—had a presence that commanded respect. His lessons often carried a reflective undertone, particularly when he spoke of mortality. With a mix of sincerity and gravity, he would remind us how fleeting and fragile life is, urging us to look beyond the material and focus on what truly matters. He would point to the towering buildings around us and say, "Look at those structures—people spend their lives building them. But when death comes, they won't even take a single brick with them to their grave." The imagery was striking, his words delivered with a calm certainty that left a lasting imprint. He extended the metaphor further, painting a vivid picture of the possessions we cling to. "Even the pillow a man sleeps on will be taken from him, the socks he wears will no longer be his. In the end, we leave this world with only our deeds—the actions we've performed, the lives we've touched." For Sir Khattak, these reminders were not morbid musings but an ethical call to action. They were an invitation to live morally, to help those in need, and to prioritize doing good over accumulating wealth or status. "We are never made for here," he would remind us, urging us to view life not as an endless pursuit of material gains but as an opportunity to cultivate kindness, integrity, and a legacy of care. His words were more than just philosophical musings—they were a guide for living with purpose. He encouraged his students to reflect on the transience of life not with despair but with determination, to ensure that the inevitable end was met with the comfort of knowing one had lived meaningfully.

Throughout history, the lives of great figures have often been marked by an intimate proximity to death. Whether as warriors, conquerors, or philosophers, their stories reveal not only their aspirations but also their struggles with mortality—a force that no power, fame, or conquest could overcome.

Khalid Bin Waleed: The Warrior Who Sought a Glorious End

Khalid Bin Waleed, one of history's most celebrated military strategists, earned the title "Sword of Allah" for his unmatched prowess on the battlefield. His victories were legendary, and his tactical genius reshaped the course of empires. Yet, beneath the armor and triumphs lay a man deeply reflective of life's ultimate truth: death.

"I witnessed such and such battles, and there is no place on my body the size of a handspan that has not received a blow from a sword or been pierced by an arrow or spear. But here I am, dying on my bed as a camel dies. May the cowards never prosper. I sought death in the places where it may be sought, but it was only decreed that I should die on my own bed." [Siyar A'laam An-Nubula', 1/382]"

Despite a lifetime of victories, Khalid yearned for a death that mirrored his life—a martyr's end on the battlefield, where honor and valor converged. He longed for his final breath to be taken amidst the chaos of war, a testament to his dedication to his cause. Yet, fate decreed otherwise. Khalid's death came not on the battlefield but in the quiet of his bed, a contrast that deeply unsettled him. In his final moments, Khalid reportedly lamented that his body bore scars from countless battles, yet none of them had led to the death he so desired. His reflections encapsulate the warrior's paradox: a life defined by courage and victory, yet haunted by the unfulfilled yearning for a meaningful end. Khalid's story reminds us that even the mightiest among us are bound by the unpredictability of mortality.

Alexander the Great, the Macedonian king who built one of the largest empires in history, lived a life of relentless ambition. By the age of 30, he had conquered vast swathes of the known world, from Greece to India, driven by a vision of immortality through glory and legacy. Yet, his encounters with mortality—both his own and that of others—revealed the limits of human aspiration. One of the most poignant moments in Alexander's life came when he ordered his men to dig an empty grave in his camp, a stark reminder to himself and his army of life's transience. Despite his conquests, Alexander was keenly aware of the impermanence of power and the inevitability of death. His early demise at the age of 32 underscored this truth, leaving behind an empire that crumbled as quickly as it was built. Alexander's story serves as a timeless lesson: no matter how vast one's achievements, the fragility of human life remains an unalterable reality. His pursuit of immortality through empire was ultimately humbled by the truth that death spares no one—not even the greatest of kings.

The lives of Khalid Bin Waleed and Alexander the Great highlight a profound philosophical truth: death is the ultimate equalizer, but it is also what gives life its urgency and meaning. Without the inevitability of an end, life's choices, ambitions, and relationships would lose their depth. To grapple with mortality is to confront life's most essential question: how should one live? For Khalid, the answer lay in living with honor and purpose, while Alexander sought meaning through legacy and achievement. Both men, in their own ways, exemplified the human desire to transcend death—not by denying it but by living so fully that their lives would echo through history. Philosophers have long posited that the awareness of death urges individuals to live with authenticity. Existentialist thinkers like Søren Kierkegaard and Martin Heidegger emphasized that facing one's mortality can liberate individuals from trivial concerns, enabling them to focus on what truly matters: love, creativity, morality, and connection. In this light, the proximity to death that marked the lives of Khalid and Alexander was not a burden but a profound teacher. It shaped their choices, illuminated their values, and left legacies that continue to inspire. The stories of Khalid Bin Waleed and Alexander the Great offer profound lessons about mortality—not as an ending to fear, but as a force that gives life its urgency and meaning. Their lives, shaped by proximity to death, illuminate a truth that resonates across time: to confront mortality is to learn the art of living. Mortality, far from being a grim specter, is a teacher that strips away the distractions of life, revealing what truly matters. When we reflect on death—not in despair, but in earnest acknowledgment—we are reminded of life's fleeting nature. This awareness urges us to focus on the present, to prioritize the enduring over the ephemeral. Philosophers have long turned to mortality as a guide. The Stoics, with their practice of *memento mori* ("remember you will die"), believed that contemplating death fosters clarity and purpose. Marcus Aurelius urged, *"You could leave life right now. Let that determine what you do and say and think."* This was not a call to fear death but to live deliberately, ensuring that one's actions aligned with one's values. Similarly, in Buddhist philosophy, the impermanence of life is seen as a source of wisdom. Recognizing that everything—our possessions, relationships, and even our own existence—is transient fosters gratitude and compassion. It sharpens our understanding that life's fragility is precisely what makes it precious.

Khalid Bin Waleed's yearning for a warrior's death and Alexander the Great's quest for immortality through legacy highlight the human desire to transcend the limits of time. Yet, their stories also serve as reminders that true immortality lies not in denying death but in living so meaningfully that one's impact endures. When we allow mortality to guide us, we learn to live with intention. The inevitability of death teaches us to value the small, fleeting moments—those quiet connections with loved ones, the satisfaction of meaningful work, the beauty of a sunrise. It compels us to reconcile with what we fear and to cherish what we have, understanding that every moment counts. In this way, mortality becomes not a burden but a gift. It pushes us to say the words that need saying, to take the risks that truly matter, and to craft a life of authenticity and purpose. By embracing the finite, we find the infinite value in the here and now. As Khalid, Alexander, and countless others have shown, the proximity to death does not diminish life—it elevates it. To live with the awareness of mortality is to transform fear into focus, hesitation into action, and existence into legacy. It is to understand that while death is certain, the meaning we create in life is boundless.

Mortality, as an inescapable aspect of the human condition, embodies a profound paradox. On one hand, the inevitability of death stirs deep-seated fear and anxiety—a primal instinct rooted in our desire to preserve life. On the other, this very awareness can act as a liberating force, encouraging us to live more authentically, courageously, and meaningfully. Death, then, is both an adversary and a teacher, simultaneously dreaded and revered. The duality of death lies at the heart of its paradox. For many, the thought of an inevitable end is suffused with dread. It confronts us with our vulnerability, the loss of control, and the erasure of identity. This fear often leads to denial or avoidance, as we seek distractions in the mundane and the material to shield ourselves from confronting mortality. Yet, paradoxically, death also offers a unique kind of freedom. It strips away the illusions of permanence and the pretense of invulnerability, forcing us to face life's raw and unvarnished truths. By doing so, it liberates us from trivial concerns and compels us to focus on what truly matters—our values, relationships, and the legacy we wish to leave behind.

Philosophers across centuries have grappled with the question of how the awareness of mortality shapes human choices and behavior. Existentialists like Jean-Paul Sartre and Martin Heidegger argue that the recognition of death is central to living authentically. Heidegger's concept of *being-toward-death* suggests that only by confronting our finitude can we truly appreciate the richness of existence and take responsibility for our lives. Conversely, the fear of death can also paralyze. It manifests in behaviors aimed at avoidance—pursuits of pleasure, accumulation of wealth, or clinging to routines that provide a false sense of security. This avoidance, while comforting in the short term, often leads to a life that is shallow and unfulfilled, detached from the deeper questions of purpose and meaning. In shaping human relationships, mortality often acts as both a bridge and a barrier. The knowledge that our time with loved ones is limited can deepen our connections, making us more present and appreciative. At the same time, the fear of losing others—or of being lost ourselves—can create walls of emotional distance, as we attempt to shield ourselves from the pain of inevitable loss.

The paradox of mortality raises profound existential dilemmas. Should we live in constant awareness of our inevitable end, striving for meaning and depth in every action? Or should we ignore death's shadow, focusing instead on immediate pleasure and comfort? Living with the awareness of mortality is both a challenge and an opportunity. It demands courage to face life's fragility, yet it also offers the gift of perspective. To live fully in the face of death is to recognize that time is finite, that each moment carries the weight of irreplaceability. This recognition can inspire a life of greater intention, where we prioritize what truly aligns with our deepest values. Ignoring mortality, on the other hand, may shield us from existential anxiety but at the cost of depth and authenticity. A life lived in denial of death risks being superficial, driven by fleeting distractions rather than enduring purpose. Perhaps the key to resolving this paradox lies in embracing death not as an end to be feared but as a teacher to be heeded. To confront mortality is to confront the impermanence of all things, a truth that can unshackle us from illusions of permanence and control. This confrontation, though unsettling, has the potential to reveal life's true essence. An authentic life—a life lived courageously and meaningfully—arises from this confrontation. When we accept that nothing lasts forever, we are freed from the fear of losing what we have. This freedom allows us to cherish the present, to take risks worth taking, and to pursue paths aligned with our inner truths rather than external expectations. The paradox of mortality, then, is not a contradiction to be resolved but a duality to be embraced. Fear and freedom, anxiety and enlightenment—these are the twin forces that shape our existence. By walking the tightrope between them, we learn not just to face death but to live in its light, with clarity, purpose, and the courage to be fully alive.

As I reflect on my parents' wishes, it becomes clear how deeply mortality shapes our desires and actions. My parents, particularly as they grew older, often expressed a quiet but profound longing: to see their children happy, settled, and well-cared for before they passed. This wasn't just about securing material success for us, but about ensuring that their presence, their love, and their values would live on in some way. For them, the idea of legacy wasn't just an abstract concept but a tangible desire to leave a part of themselves in the world, a part that could continue even after they were gone. I could see in their eyes, especially as they grew older, a desire for continuity. They wanted to know that the love, the guidance, and the sacrifices they had given would have lasting effects. Watching us grow, thrive, and find fulfillment in our own lives was, for them, a kind of immortality. This, I realized, is a universal truth: death, with all its finality, compels us to seek something that will outlast our physical existence.

This desire to transcend death often manifests through our children. Parents don't just want their children to succeed; they want to see their values, their dreams, their essence carried forward in the next generation. It's as if, in seeing their children settled and fulfilled, parents feel that their journey is not over, that their life's purpose has been passed on. In the same way, many of us seek to leave something meaningful behind—whether through family, work, or the impact we have on others. We all long to create something that survives us, something that says, *I was here, and I mattered*. This impulse is deeply philosophical. When faced with the reality of death, we search for ways to endure beyond our bodies. For some, it's through raising children who carry on the family name or traditions. For others, it might be through contributing to society in ways that will have a ripple effect for generations. Legacy becomes a way to ensure that we don't simply fade into nothingness, that some part of us remains in the world, having made a difference. But death doesn't just motivate us to leave behind something physical or permanent. It also serves as a powerful catalyst for creating meaning in our lives.

The awareness of our finite time on Earth compels us to act with purpose, to live with care, and to build something that reflects our truest selves. Legacy becomes more than just a collection of possessions or accomplishments; it is the essence of who we are, embodied in our relationships, our work, and the impact we have on the lives of others. I've come to understand that the desire for legacy is not about trying to avoid death or to achieve immortality. It's about living in a way that acknowledges our mortality, yet rises above it. It's about knowing that time is precious, that every moment counts, and that what we leave behind will be a reflection of how we spent that time. Parents, in their wishes for their children, embody this desire for continuity. They want to know that their lives—filled with love, sacrifice, and care—have mattered. And in the lives of their children, they see the living, breathing evidence of that meaning. Reflecting on this desire for legacy brings a sense of responsibility. It reminds me that my actions today, my choices, my love, my work—they all play a part in the legacy I will leave. It's not just about what I create, but how I live, how I show up in the world, and how I make others feel. Legacy isn't just about what survives us; it's about how we live with intention, knowing that our time is limited and that everything we do has the potential to leave a lasting impact. Through this lens, mortality no longer feels like something to fear, but something to honor—a force that drives us to live fully, to give of ourselves, and to build something that will carry our essence beyond the grave. There is a fear of death that goes beyond the terror of the end itself, a "due fear" that arises from the very awareness that our time on this Earth is finite. This fear, though often uncomfortable, is not simply a fear of dying but a deep recognition that life, with all its joys and trials, is temporary. It is a fear that calls us to attention, urging us to make the most of the limited time we have. It is a reminder that our days are numbered, and with that awareness comes an undeniable urge to live well, to act with purpose, and to seek meaning in all that we do. This recognition of mortality becomes a moral compass, steering us toward a life that is not just about survival, but about living with intention. The knowledge that life is short pushes us to ask: How do we want to be remembered? What kind of impact do we wish to have? The fear of death, when acknowledged, can drive us to be our best selves, to strive for kindness, justice, and goodness, knowing that each moment could be our last.

The question of why we strive to be good, just, and kind often echoes in our minds. Is it because we seek a reward in the afterlife, or is there something inherent in the recognition of our own mortality that pushes us toward these virtues? I believe it is both. The awareness of death brings clarity, urging us to act in ways that reflect the best of humanity. We are reminded that our lives are not just about personal achievement or accumulation, but about contributing to the greater good. Philosophically, this idea has been explored throughout history. The Stoics, for instance, believed that an understanding of death was essential for virtuous living. Marcus Aurelius, in his meditations, often reflected on how the certainty of death should guide us to live with virtue, honesty, and integrity. For him, life's fragility demanded a response: to live morally, not just for ourselves, but for the good of others and the world around us. Death forces us to reckon with our limitations as human beings. We know we cannot escape it, and in this inevitable truth lies the opportunity to live more meaningfully. It becomes clear that our actions—how we treat others, how we contribute to society, how we live according to our principles—are what will define us in the end. The awareness of our mortality encourages us to focus on what really matters, to act with care and responsibility, knowing that time is a gift that is not guaranteed. This "due fear" of death, then, becomes a catalyst for living with greater authenticity. It is a fear that does not paralyze us but compels us to act in ways that reflect our highest values. It is the fear that leads us to ask the hard questions about the kind of legacy we wish to leave behind. How can we live in such a way that we make a meaningful difference, both in the lives of others and in the world? How can we ensure that our time here has not been wasted, that we have lived with purpose and love? Ultimately, death, in its stark and inevitable presence, pushes us to make our lives meaningful. It forces us to confront the reality that we are finite beings with limited time, and in doing so, it challenges us to transcend the ordinary and aim for the extraordinary. The fear of death becomes, not an obstacle, but a powerful force that drives us to live fully, to give of ourselves, and to create a life that is rich in purpose, meaning, and connection.

In the end, it becomes clear that the act of acknowledging death transforms the very way we live. The awareness of our mortality, rather than casting a shadow over our existence, illuminates it. It encourages us to cherish the fleeting moments, to approach life with gratitude, and to be fully present in each experience. Recognizing that life is impermanent opens our eyes to the beauty in the ordinary, the depth in relationships, and the importance of living authentically. It is only through understanding that our time is finite that we can truly appreciate the gift of life. The "due fear" of death, far from being a paralyzing force, serves as a motivating one. It is not a fear that seeks to control or limit us but one that urges us to act with intention, to live with purpose, and to prioritize what truly matters. This fear reminds us that life is fragile, and in its fragility lies the imperative to make every moment count. By embracing this fear, we learn not to avoid it but to let it fuel us to live courageously—making choices that reflect our values and connecting with others in meaningful ways. Ultimately, to live without fear of death is to live without fully appreciating life. When we deny or ignore the reality of mortality, we may squander the precious time we have, distracted by what is trivial or fleeting. But by embracing the "due fear," we are reminded that each day is a gift—an opportunity to live authentically, to contribute to the world, and to leave behind a legacy of meaning and love. It is through the recognition of life's impermanence that we find the clarity and motivation to live more fully, to be more present, and to make our lives matter. In this light, death is not an enemy to be feared but a companion that teaches us how to live. By acknowledging it, we unlock the potential to live with greater mindfulness, deeper gratitude, and a heightened sense of purpose. Each breath, each moment, becomes more precious because we know it is not forever. And in this knowing, we find the courage to embrace life—finiteness and all.

Chapter 8

At Last

"In the heart of the modern city, where the sub-man is trapped in the endless cycle of consumption and burnout, we see a world ruled by overproduction, speed, and an insatiable desire for more. Yet, as Byung-Chul Han warns, this "hyperactive" existence leads not to freedom, but to a quiet exhaustion, a weariness of the soul. It is here that the law of nature, as Thoreau saw it, calls us back to simplicity—the very essence of being. For in the relentless complexity of modern life, we lose sight of what is truly essential. The sub-man is not free, but shackled by his own desires, while nature's simplicity offers the only path to genuine freedom: a return to what is vital, unadorned, and true. The more we consume, the less we live. Only in simplicity, in stripping away the superfluous, can one find the clarity of mind and the depth of spirit that our age has forgotten."

SubHuman

We are free. We cannot deny this freedom, as it is an inescapable part of being human. According to existentialist philosopher Simone de Beauvoir, any attempt to escape freedom is illusory, as such attempts are also a choice and, therefore, an act of freedom.

Yet, some people try to run away from this freedom, as it frightens them. By doing so, they evade responsibility, refusing to engage with life and make it a meaningful endeavor. They hide in the shadows; they negate themselves; they stand for nothing and easily fall for anything. According to Beauvoir, this makes such individuals dangerous, as they are easily manipulated by forces that would love to use them as pawns. We are talking here about the subhuman. The existentialist subhuman is not a neckbearded short guy with a weak chin living in his mom's basement. For Beauvoir, the subhuman is an archetypical position toward what she called "the ambiguity of freedom." This concept is the central theme of her book *The Ethics of Ambiguity*, one of the foundational texts of existentialism. For Simone de Beauvoir, freedom is a double-edged sword: a gift and a burden. The bad news is that life comes with limitations—things that are a given, "fate," if you will. The good news is we have the freedom to act despite these things, and many limitations can be overcome. We are, thus, allowed to shape our lives authentically to an extent: there is a space, and that space is freedom. But some people deny this freedom and the opportunity to forge their authentic path. They do not want it, as it scares them, and so they hide from it in curious ways. Beauvoir argued that such people fall into two categories: the subhuman and the serious person.

Please note I took the existentialist freedom to use the term "subhuman" instead of Beauvoir's original term "sub-man" as a universal and ungendered version of the concept. Simone de

Beauvoir was a French existentialist philosopher born into a Parisian bourgeois family. Her father encouraged her intellectual development. As she was good at it, he ironically but proudly exclaimed: "Simone thinks like a man." Little did he know that she would later become one of the most important figures in feminist thought, writing the groundbreaking work *The Second Sex.* She had a lifelong partnership with none other than Jean-Paul Sartre. They were quite the unconventional couple: they had an open relationship based on respecting each other's freedom, which coincided with their philosophy. The turmoil of World War II and the challenges of that era deepened Beauvoir's reflections on themes like freedom, meaning, and responsibility, inspiring her later works, such as *The Ethics of Ambiguity.* In this book, Beauvoir explores how to live genuinely in a world without ready-made meaning. She saw life's freedom as a privilege but also a responsibility. It is a game that must be played. Whatever we do, we are always part of that game, even if we refuse to play and sit on the sidelines. What does it mean to be free? Simone de Beauvoir believed that freedom is inherently ambiguous—we are both free and not free. On the one hand, we are subjects who can make choices and create meaning in life. On the other hand, we are objects to others and are embedded in a world shaped by circumstances beyond our control. Consider a talented painter with a strong drive to create. She has the materials, space, and income from her day job, so nothing stops her from painting and finding meaning in her work. Yet, she faces constraints: a lack of recognition, financial pressure, and a world more captivated by Netflix than art galleries. Then, a war breaks out, forcing her to enlist in the military and abandon her art. In this example, we see how the ambiguity of freedom comes with a constant tension between freedom and "facticity," the latter meaning the "facts" of our situation. Facticity is a set of conditions—circumstances that shape our lives. For the painter, it's her financial situation, global conflicts, and societal trends. Many of these things cannot be changed, but some of them can be overcome. Suppose the painter is an existentialist. As an existentialist, she doesn't just passively allow herself to be shaped by circumstances. If she did, she would be merely an object, a product entirely formed by outside forces. An existentialist embraces both object and subject, meaning the painter actively shapes her life (and, simultaneously, the world) despite the facts of her situation. This dynamic creates tension: it's subject versus object, imposing versus being imposed on, creating purpose versus becoming subjected to someone else's. According to Beauvoir, embracing freedom means transcending one's facticity and forging an authentic path despite it. I admit this sounds pretty vague. So, the question is: how do we pull this off? The answer is complicated. Beauvoir does not provide fixed morals or ethics to guide us on the path of freedom because freedom is subjective. An individual's freedom depends on their unique circumstances. It's personal and theirs to decide. True freedom implies a triumph over facticity—overcoming the obstacles in the way of one's authentic path. Yet, this struggle is different for everyone because everyone's situation is different. If you aim to be free and then follow some step-by-step guide on how to get that freedom written by, let's say, someone on YouTube, you're essentially giving up your freedom. You just surrender yourself to someone else's blueprint for what life should be like. In the existentialist sense, true freedom means figuring out one's own direction in life and actively choosing it. An ethics of ambiguity, therefore, can never be universal, or as Beauvoir states:

"An ethics of ambiguity will be one which will refuse to deny a priori that separate existents can, at the same time, be bound to each other, that their individual freedoms can forge laws valid for all." But does acknowledging our freedom mean we can do anything we want? For Beauvoir, freedom implies responsibility. The world influences and constrains us, but our actions also shape it. If we remain passive, external forces dictate our lives. We are mere objects of our circumstances in that case. But the moment we transcend our conditions and act freely, we impact ourselves and others. Thus, we must choose responsibly. Our choices will affect people, whether we like it or not. For example, a teacher shaping young minds must recognize their influence and see it as their responsibility to encourage critical thinking and empathy, rather than imposing personal biases or fostering ignorance. Keeping this in mind, let's examine Beauvoir's archetypical attitudes that deny freedom. So, what's a subhuman? Before this archetype makes sense, we'll have to dive a bit deeper into what Beauvoir believes is the origin of one's attitude toward ambiguity: childhood.

"The child's situation is characterized by his finding

himself cast into a universe which he has not helped to establish, which has been fashioned without him, and which appears to him as an absolute to which he can only submit. In his eyes, human inventions, words, customs, and values are given facts, as inevitable as the sky and the trees."

When we're still children, we're not aware of the ambiguity of freedom, which is a natural thing, says Beauvoir. Our parents are godlike, and so are our teachers. To children, the adult world is serious: these big people know what life is all about; they hold the absolute truth about the world.
"My momma says…" Well, whatever it is, it's true.

The child himself isn't serious. He's safely living under the eyes of the adults, irresponsibly carefree. Someday, he'll be part of the "seriousness," and the absolute world will be accessible to him.

Of course, adults do not have a monopoly on wisdom, and their values and morals are not absolute. As children grow older, they may become aware of how unfounded the adult world is. Mom's truisms about how girls are supposed to become mothers and how boys are not supposed to cry—these used to be the absolute truth, but now they sound questionable. Like… why? Who says so? Suddenly, the child realizes there are no fixed roles and laws. Beauvoir famously stated, "One is not born, but rather becomes, a woman." Hence, she could very well choose not to. From the existentialist viewpoint, we are nothingness. Existence precedes essence. We come into this world as empty canvases, subjected to an ambiguous freedom. More often than not, this empty, open, and contingent universe in front of them scares people. As children, things were still simple and absolute. As adults, the ambivalence and uncertainty of it all become apparent. Here's where the archetype of the "serious man" or "serious person" comes in, which is, according to Beauvoir, most people's attitude. The serious person denies his freedom. He wants to get rid of it.

"The serious man gets rid of his freedom by claiming to subordinate it to values which would be unconditioned. He imagines that the accession to these values likewise permanently confers value upon himself."

The serious person is devoted to what he deems a higher purpose that justifies his existence. He seeks identity and meaning in predefined roles, giving him an illusion of absolute purpose and truth. To maintain this illusion, he willingly throws critical thinking overboard. He wants to lose himself in these external entities. Why? Because by doing so, he doesn't have to think for himself anymore. Big Daddy does it for him, just as his parents did when he was a kid. Now, which roles are we talking about? It could be anything. Take a mid-level manager, for example, who is basically everyone's pain in the ass. His identity is almost entirely submerged in the company. His holy book? The company's code of ethics. The sacred symbol he proudly carries on his suitcase? The company's logo. Not to mention the whiteboard in his bedroom showing the company's mission statement and future growth plan... Okay, this sounds

224

hyperbolic, but seriously (pun intended), most people seek something external to become a meaning-giving entity. They lose themselves in roles—soldiers, fathers, professors, you name it—and the values these roles entail. Take a serious person assuming the role of a student, for example. Instead of being merely someone who studies, he begins to act, think, and talk like a stereotypical studious automaton or an archetypical frat boy. He sacrifices his authenticity, but who cares? He's now part of the Borg—a safe system that provides stability and a sense of purpose. In this way, the serious person becomes a textbook NPC, moving through life on autopilot and following a script dictated by external values.

The serious person seems selfless, sacrificing himself for the greater good. But there's a catch: what truly matters to him isn't so much the cause itself but the opportunity to lose himself in it. It's an existential lifebuoy, offering certainty and escape from the ambiguity of freedom. The serious person clings to childhood absolutes: the time when values imposed by authority figures felt unquestionable. Beauvoir warns this attitude can lead to tyranny, as the serious person prioritizes their chosen system over humanity. For example, someone overly committed to an ideology is likely to ignore the humanity of others, impose his beliefs as absolute truths, and justify harm and oppression in the name of his cause. However, the serious person can also lose his cause. One day, his system of absolutes could collapse, and he risks sliding into another archetype: the subhuman. What does it mean to be a subhuman? For some, the term "subhuman" sounds familiar, as it's a term used by the incel (or involuntary celibate) subculture to describe men that are inferior in terms of physical appearance and status. Beauvoir's meaning of subhuman is fundamentally different. From her viewpoint, the subhuman has nothing to do with not having a well-defined jawline. It has nothing to do with being ugly or from a certain "race." Genetics are irrelevant. Sure, they are a given fact of life that we cannot change, and they may constrain us in certain areas. But they do not restrict the subjectivity of our existence. In other words, we can still create meaning despite our constraints. The subhuman rejects freedom, unlike the serious person, who surrenders it to external values. He drifts through life, letting circumstances like genetics or class define him. They cope through distractions—video games, television, social media. This mindset overlaps with incels, who fatalistically believe their situation is hopeless. Facticity is everything. "It's over" is their mantra. Beauvoir warns that the subhuman is also dangerous. Not only is he passive and indifferent in the face of injustice, but he's also an easy target for tyrants and oppressive systems. They adopt ideologies passively, becoming tools for others' agendas. As Beauvoir states:

"One day, a monarchist, the next day, an anarchist, he is more readily anti-semitic, anti-clerical, or anti-republican. Thus, though we have defined him as a denial and a flight, the sub-man is not a harmless creature. He realizes himself in the world as a blind uncontrolled force which anybody can get control of.

*In lynchings, in pogroms, in all the great bloody
movements organized by the fanaticism of seriousness
and passion, movements where there is no risk, those
who do the actual dirty work are recruited from
among the sub-men."*

From Beauvoir's perspective, not choosing is still a
choice—and a dangerous one. But there's always a
way out. For most of us, freedom is within reach,
waiting to be claimed. In *The Ethics of Ambiguity,*
Beauvoir explores how to deal with the complexities
of freedom: how to become an existentialist.

Emptier

Many ages ago, there was Sisyphus, a cunning king
who made the mistake of challenging the gods. His
punishment was simple but torturous: the gods
condemned him to push a massive boulder up a hill,
only for it to roll back down each time he reached the
top. As his punishment was eternal, he had to repeat
this process daily. Sisyphus, therefore, found himself
trapped in an empty, meaningless life of toil. As
modern-day Sisyphuses, aren't we condemned to a
similar fate? Aren't we stuck in a relentless grind, our
lives reduced to endless tasks? Could it be that, as
subjects of an achievement society, we're losing
something essential? Could it be that, in our constant
productivity and pursuit of achievement, we've
forgotten to live? In his book *The Scent of Time: A
Philosophical Essay on the Art of Lingering*, Korean-
born German philosopher Byung-Chul Han explains
that, in our fast-paced world, we experience time in a
fundamentally different way. Time has become

atomized, causing it to lack direction, coherence, and meaning. As we hop from one event to another, none of these events carry depth or significance. According to Han, we experience a temporal crisis, which causes us to feel restless, anxious, nervous, and frantic. But there's hope for recovery, which Han also shares in his book. According to Han, today's society demands that people achieve, and failing to perform makes you a "loser." Achievement has become an ultimate concern—a virtue—leading us to constantly 'whip' ourselves into productivity. In his book *The Burnout Society*, Han describes the workings of the achievement society and its destructive consequences, such as anxiety and burnout. While the imperative to achieve primarily touches upon our working lives (such as chasing financial success or becoming startup entrepreneurs), the collective accomplishment-driven attitude also bleeds into the remainder of our lives, which we could classify as 'leisure.' Even leisure has become some form of achievement. How we generally fill our free time has become a matter of checking boxes. For example, when we travel, we try to cram as many activities as possible into our schedules, rushing from place to place, like warehouse workers rushing from shelf to shelf, picking orders. The general experience of traveling often lacks reflection, digestion, and simply being there. Experiencing it is more akin to window shopping. Many people today are more interested in whether a particular place is "Instagrammable" than in whether there's some profound, meaningful experience to find. Even watching a TV series has become a matter of quantity. In the past, certain shows created shared excitement—we'd talk about them beforehand, watch them together, and reminisce afterward. The experience extended beyond the airing itself. Today, most entertainment is available on demand. There's much less anticipation, excitement for what's to come, and collective experience. And because the entertainment options are so abundant, we tend to move on immediately to the next instead of adequately digesting and reflecting on what we just consumed. Nowadays, dating also shows a societal shift from quality to quantity. Where marriage and commitment were once the norm, serial monogamy (and even polyamory) has become more prevalent. We prefer more, different experiences—superficially and fleetingly—over actual depth and meaning in relationships. From today's perspective, depth and length in relationships also come with monotony and boredom, things we now look down upon and aim to avoid. Why waste time in the repetitiveness of long-term commitments if we can have exciting honeymoon phases characterized by novelty every couple of years with a new person? Today's dominant mode of living is marked by relentless activity. Han refers to it as *vita activa* (the active life), a term coined initially by Hannah Arendt to describe a life focused on labor, work, and action. Han criticizes the contemporary form of *vita activa* in the context of modern capitalism and the achievement society, as he observes that activity has become an end in itself. Being active or 'in pursuit' is what makes our lives count. There's no place for contemplation or reflection. There's no place for what Han calls the "duration" of time. Not producing or pursuing some kind of goal is seen as wasteful. At the root of our current "age of haste" lies a fear of missing out. This fear leans on the idea that, to make our lives more fulfilled and richer in experience, we must escalate the quantity of experience. In other words, the more experiences we can stuff into our lifespans, the better. Of course, doing so requires an acceleration in savoring worldly experiences. We want to do more different things in a shorter period. However, according to Han, such a pursuit is counterproductive:

"Whoever tries to live faster will ultimately also die faster. It is not the total number of events, but the experience of duration which makes life more fulfilling. Where one event follows close on the heels of another, nothing enduring comes about. Fulfillment and meaning cannot be explained on quantitative grounds."

A life that is lived quickly, without anything lasting long and without anything slow, a life characterized by quick, short-term, and short-lived experiences, is itself a short life, no matter how high the "rate of experience" may be.

According to Han, our fast-paced lives give way to franticness, restlessness, nervousness, and anxiety. But more profoundly, as he describes in his book, our relationship with time has changed; time has lost its "scent." People often say, "Things were better in days gone by." But looking at the statistics regarding things like wealth, physical health, and overall safety, we could hardly make that case. Still, there's something about the old days, something we've lost when life became more fast-paced, individualistic, and achievement-driven. According to Han, our "age of haste" is like a cinematographic succession of point-like presences without access to beauty or truth. We want immediate enjoyment, and the default response to enjoyment fading is moving on to the next. As we pursue a larger quantity and variety of experiences in an attempt to enrich our lives, time also moves faster. Moreover, as Han explains, we experience time as temporal points, which he calls "atomized time." Atomized time is a discontinuous time. There is nothing to bind events together and thus found a connection, a duration. Atomized time fragments life into a directionless sequence of isolated moments, leaving no space for cohesion or meaningful conclusions. Without a narrative connecting past, present, and future, experiences remain shallow and fleeting. Han explains that time used to be more structured. For example, in prehistoric times, time was cyclical, and we would adapt to these cycles, such as the seasons and lunar phases. Time had a rhythm, which granted us stability and predictability. Later, religion provided us with meaning through a greater narrative. God gave us purpose and guidelines by which to live. Whatever we did, as religious people, everything fit into a larger narrative. According to Han, actual profound experience lies in vast temporal spaces. Unlike point-time (or atomized time), these more significant periods consist of a dialectic between past and future, experienced in the present. These temporal spaces allow for a sense of continuity and depth. Religion, for instance, gives our lives a special purpose. It creates an overarching narrative, a defined purpose, and a "why" to everything we do. For example, an Abrahamic religion such as Islam provides a rhythm of rituals and celebrations. Take Ramadan, for example—a period of fasting from sunrise to sunset, during which Muslims experience shared meaning and conclude with a celebration. As a recurring holy month, Ramadan gives time rhythm. It takes people out of atomized time into a world of meaning. A day of fasting isn't just an isolated point in time; it's part of something bigger, combining past, present, and future. Han stated: *God functions like a stabilizer of time. He ensures a lasting, perennial present.* However, the regime has changed. For a significant part of the world, God lost His power. This hasn't been without consequences, says Han, as God's "death" (referring to Nietzsche) deprived time of any theological meaning, any doctrine of design and purpose. In postmodernity, the present has shrunk to a fleeting point in time, atomized and disconnected from any meaningful past or future.

"Atomization and individualization take hold of societies as a whole. Social practices such as promising, fidelity, or commitment, which are temporal practices in the sense that they commit to a future and thus limit the horizon of the future, thus founding duration, are all losing their importance."

What depth do our lives have if we jump from moment to moment? According to Han, atomized time doesn't allow us to complete anything. Take serial monogamy, for example, which characterizes itself not just by alternating relationships but also, from my own observations, by very small in-betweens and often no in-betweens at all. According to Han, a meaningful conclusion is necessary for proper experience. Experience isn't just about the activity itself—it involves anticipation, reflection, and a narrative that connects it to something greater. It's a bit like Lao Tzu's cup: the emptiness within and around it gives it purpose. Similarly, without the space around our actions—time to linger and reflect—this pointed, atomized time reduces life to isolated tasks, leaving no room for genuine experience, no room for completion or transition to the next. We prefer not to endure these intervals as we hop from one possibility to another. After all, these transitional phases are a waste of time, obstructing us from more consumption and achievement. However, Han states that intervals—periods of not achieving and pursuing—serve a function. They provide us with direction and cohesion. They bring order. For example, religious celebrations are intervals that provide us with structure, and so are rites of passage, as they close off one life chapter and transition to the next. Without these intervals, time becomes chaotic, a space without direction. Things may have been better in the days gone by because our relationship with time was different. Events had more gravity and space around them. Time was slower. As we anticipated and completed something and transitioned into the next, we experienced more depth. Commitments were sacred; friendships were longer and deeper. We could commit to a board game with family and friends for a whole evening, feeling genuine connection and fulfillment instead of checking hundreds of TikTok reels on our smartphones, which leaves us empty, restless, and unfulfilled. As times have changed, and, for many, God as a "stabilizer of time" has become something of the past, and life's pace is speeding up exponentially, what can we do to reclaim time? Han proposes a path to recovery: the art of lingering. In a world obsessed with productivity, where rushing and multitasking have become the new normal, and where anxiety, burnout, and depression have become prevalent, the idea of slowing sounds pretty rebellious. As *vita activa* is our dominant mode of living, being less active is akin to blasphemy. But Han wrote quite early in the book that what's necessary to overcome the temporal crisis is a revitalization of the *vita contemplativa* as a counterbalance to the *vita activa*. "The temporal crisis will only be overcome once the *vita activa*, in the midst of its crisis, again incorporates the *vita contemplativa*." According to Han, the return of the *vita contemplativa* will bring back the "scent" to time, as it liberates human beings from the compulsion of labor. But doing so requires a different look toward what we regard as "leisure." Han observes that today's leisure time is merely a break from work, as all energy is fully absorbed by work, so the only thing we do during leisure time is passive entertainment or recreation. Our free time is merely a matter of recuperating to enable us to work again with full strength. Therefore, leisure is part of work; it serves our primary purpose: labor. It's not contemplative rest, which Han regards as true leisure, disconnected from work.

So, what's *vita contemplativa* or the art of lingering? What does contemplation actually mean? In his book,

Han guides us through different views of contemplation and its proper place in our lives by philosophers such as Hannah Arendt, Martin Heidegger, and Aristotle. In my own words, the essence of Han's *vita contemplativa* (which is deeply tied to our relationship with time) is this: instead of using time, linger in it. Leisure isn't a mere break to recover from working; it is a space to endure, reflect, and simply be. In the *vita contemplativa*, time becomes something to inhabit rather than use. For example, instead of actively directing our thoughts to achieve something, we allow them to arise naturally in moments of reflection. Traveling, for instance, transforms from a means of reaching a destination to experiencing the journey itself—wandering for the sake of wandering. This contemplative space lets us think deeply about life, truth, and the cosmos: things far beyond the trivialities of daily life. It offers room to breathe, reflect, and transition meaningfully through rituals or solitude. It's also where original ideas and profound insights emerge—possibilities that the restlessness of the *vita activa* does not allow.

"Contemplative lingering gives time," writes Han, *unlike the active life, which uses up and kills it. He states: "When life regains its capacity for contemplation, it gains in time and space, in duration and vastness."*

Simplify

Transcendentalist philosopher Henry David Thoreau argued that, for humans, simplicity is the law of nature. We thrive in simplicity: it's an optimal state free of clutter and unnecessary weight. When our lives are simple, it's easier to see where we stand, where we come from, and where we are moving, as the minimal amount of chaos troubles our vision. Thoreau compared the value of simplicity to a mathematician solving an equation; he "reduces it to its simplest terms." Because of today's many possibilities, people tend to overcomplicate life. Our consumerist culture encourages us to buy unnecessary items, instilling in us the belief that our lives are incomplete or inconvenient without them. Additionally, being part of a performance-driven and highly competitive society, our lives tend to be busy, and our goals are many. Modern life is cluttered with things, social connections, ideas, and stimuli. Worries and wishes fill our minds, and we're always restless because we fail to distinguish the forest from the trees. When immersed in complexity, it's difficult to see the essential. *"The ability to simplify means to eliminate the unnecessary so that the necessary may speak,"* stated painter Hans Hofmann. Studies suggest that there's a link between simplicity and well-being. For example, a paper published by The Centre for Development Studies at the University of Bath suggests that voluntary simplicity contributes to subjective well-being in several ways. Voluntary simplifiers report the experience of greater security, autonomy, competence, and the feeling of doing the right thing; the latter relates to ecological and societal concerns. Aside from such experiential benefits, a minimalist approach to life could lead to greater overview and living more cheaply. The ancient Greek philosopher Diogenes lived with minimal possessions, residing in a barrel on the streets, owning only some rags and a drinking cup. But when he saw a child drinking water using his hands, he threw away his drinking cup, saying, *"A child has beaten me in plainness of living."* Diogenes wasn't the only one who lived with almost no possessions. Certain hermits and various monastic orders renounce worldly possessions, partly to free themselves from the burdens that come with them. The Dalai Lama stated in an interview, *"If one's life is simple, contentment has to come. Simplicity is extremely important for happiness. Having few desires, feeling satisfied with what you have, is very vital: satisfaction with just enough food, clothing, and shelter to protect yourself from the elements."* Of course, one doesn't have to be a cynic, Buddhist monk, or hermit to experience the joys of owning less. A minimalist approach to one's possessions can make a significant difference in one's life, as it removes the unnecessary clutter our senses perceive in our immediate environment. According to Carl Jung, our living spaces are extensions of ourselves. Thus, keeping those spaces clean has a direct impact on the psyche. Also, the more stuff you own, the more you need to worry about, take care of, and protect. The fewer worries, the better one feels. The fewer things to protect, the more time and energy one saves. Also, owning less makes us more agile. We could ask ourselves what we truly need. Do we need large houses with six bedrooms and two bathrooms? Or would a smaller place suffice? Do we need an expensive car? How many of the clothes we own do we actually wear? And how many movies and television series do we watch? But pursuing stuff is tempting, as our consumerist culture promises happiness through purchase and ownership. *"Material possessions aren't great investments in contentment (as opposed to experiences)."* After the purchase, we may experience a period of euphoria that quickly subsides. Roman author and politician Pliny the Younger stated, "An object in possession seldom retains the same charm that it had in pursuit." So, if we keep our possessions minimal, we won't miss out on long-term satisfaction. Moreover, by not buying so much stuff we don't need, we don't waste money on fleeting moments of happiness while burdening ourselves with ever-increasing piles of non-essential rubbish. From a more artistically minimalist point of view, just owning less stuff is only part of the equation. A simplified and uncluttered living environment also depends on how we design it. Even though human beings are social creatures, the presence of people can serve as a significant burden. If we've surrounded ourselves with too many people, or worse, the wrong people, our social life may cause us more harm than good. The problem with having many social connections is that we often don't see which of those connections we actually enjoy. For example, we may be part of a large social circle, but within that circle, there are only a handful of people we genuinely connect with. At the same time, all those people we don't connect with expect us to attend their parties and other events. We may not even enjoy these events and see them as social obligations. With friends, quantity probably isn't better than quality. Interestingly enough, research conducted by evolutionary psychologists suggests that having fewer friends is a sign of intelligence.

SMU Associate Professor of Psychology Norman Li and evolutionary psychologist Satoshi Kanazawa of the London School of Economics conducted research which found that social interactions, even with friends, can be a problem for more intelligent people. They surveyed 15,000 people between the ages of 18 and 28, and discovered that people who live in more densely populated areas tend to report less satisfaction with their life overall. They also found that the more social interactions with close friends a person has, the greater their self-reported happiness. But there was one big exception. For more intelligent people, these correlations were diminished or even reversed.

This research shows that more social interaction correlates with greater happiness. However, these correlations are diminished or reversed for intellectuals, meaning that many social interactions make them less happy. Depending on what kind of person you are, these outcomes may be another reason to simplify your social life. The term "social minimalism" points to minimizing one's social interactions, limiting them to what's essential for one's satisfaction. Social minimalism doesn't have to mean cutting out friends or becoming a hermit, as the amount and nature of social interaction one prefers is personal. Simplifying our social lives isn't necessarily limiting the number of friends; it could also be limiting the number of social interactions with these friends and being selective about what kind of social interactions we engage in. We may avoid needless, repetitive chit-chat at specific social gatherings while embracing one-on-one conversations during forest walks. Feeling overwhelmed by our busy lives is a common complaint in modern times, which goes hand in hand with anxiety and stress. But, in many cases, it's not just because life demands too much of us; it's also because there's too much noise—mainly due to digital technology. Life is full of distractions. Especially after the arrival of modern technology, the amount of stimuli the average human being experiences is unprecedented. At any time of the day, text messages, emails, phone calls, and notifications from our countless social media pages come in. There are numerous television channels to choose from, on top of an increasing number of streaming services, and our phones grant us access to unlimited information online. Unsurprisingly, we experience a nagging feeling that there's always something to be done and that we're missing out. "Digital minimalism" is a form of minimalism concerned with limiting one's time using technology. Author Cal Newport wrote that our sociability is "too complex to be outsourced to a social network or reduced to instant messages and emojis." His book *Digital Minimalism* offers ways to declutter digitally without throwing away the baby with the bathwater. After all, technology can be very beneficial. He describes digital minimalism as follows: *"A philosophy of technology use in which you focus your online time on a small number of carefully selected and optimized activities that strongly support things you value, and then happily miss out on everything else."* By cutting down our online time, we experience far fewer unnecessary distractions and stimuli, which (considering how widespread digital technology is) amounts to a significant reduction of clutter. Indecisiveness and procrastination are illnesses of our time: an era with countless possibilities and myriad choices to make. For many, it's challenging to set priorities, as there are so many ways to go, so they want too much and focus too little. Unfortunately, if you want everything, you'll eventually end up with nothing. The schedule of the average modern-day Western individual is cramped. This mentality of "always needing to be doing something" reflects how many of today's parents raise their children. Aside from school and the occasional house chores, it's not uncommon for these kids to attend two or more different sports and several other activities a week. On Saturday, it's soccer practice; on Sunday, it's boy scouts; on Tuesday, it's tennis practice; on Wednesday, it's piano lessons; and on Thursday, it's horse riding. We see that young adults continue this trend, stuffing their schedules with many undertakings. Swiss philosopher Henri-Frederic Amiel stated, *"A man must be able to cut a knot, for everything cannot be untied; he must know how to disengage what is essential from the detail in which it is enwrapped, for everything cannot be equally considered; in a word, he must be able to simplify his duties, his business, and his life."* A minimalist approach to our schedules creates oversight and may help us concentrate on what's essential in our lives. In doing so, we need to be able to say "no" to certain things and be willing to walk in a different direction than our peers, but in exchange for more time and space in our agendas. We can declutter our environments as much as we want; if our minds are full of rubbish, then it's likely we'll still complicate our lives despite our simplified surroundings. Overthinking, worrying, and ruminating make uncomplicated things complicated. Also, it often makes problems much more significant than they are. In fact, problems originate in the mind, not in the outside world. Living a simple life while burdened by racing, complex thoughts seems pretty contradictory. Our living rooms may be minimalistic and clean, but our heads may be full of worries about work. Our agendas may be spacious, but our brains may ruminate about past events. If obsessive thinking haunts us every waking minute, despite our simplified surroundings, how futile have our efforts been to simplify our external lives for well-being? Without a doubt, an uncluttered living environment may contribute to mental clarity. But simplicity is best served with the coolness of a tranquil mind.

Chapter 9

My Statement

"As Dostoevsky once said, "Without God, everything is permitted." To live without belief in God is to cast aside any higher law and instead chart one's own course, relying solely on one's own means, desires, and reason. In doing so, one places oneself above the very order of existence, as though the weight of the universe rests on the shoulders of man alone. But God is not the mistake of humanity; He is a testament—one that will not be revealed in haste, but in the fullness of time. Let time, with its trials and revelations, prove the existence of God, for in the end, the truth is not something to be grasped immediately, but something that unfolds gradually, like the dawning of light after a long, suffocating night."

Throughout the thousands of years of human history, all the servants and messengers of God came with one consistent message: that there is a God, a higher power governing all creation. Beyond this, there was no other fundamental point of view from them. This unanimous testimony across generations and cultures further underscores the idea that belief in God is not a construct of human imagination but a universal truth revealed repeatedly to guide us.

First and foremost, it's important to understand one fundamental truth: God has always been there. This is my perspective on why I believe in God, and while I cannot convince you to adopt this belief, I can only share how I see it. We can even approach this idea logically and mathematically. Consider the universal truths that are already established—truths that form the foundation of our existence and the order of the universe. These truths, in their perfection and constancy, point toward something greater than ourselves, something eternal. Take something as simple and foundational as 2+2=4. This is a universal truth. If anyone tries to make it 5 or 3, they would clearly be wrong. Even if someone re-invents the wheel, this mathematical truth would still hold. Similarly, it's been universally established that our universe had a beginning—it didn't always exist. At one point, there was a theory called the "Steady State Theory," proposed by Fred Hoyle, Herman Bondi, and Thomas Gold in 1948. This theory suggested that the universe had no beginning or end, and it had existed in a steady, unchanging state forever. However, this theory has since been disproven and is no longer accepted. In fact, the downfall of the Steady State Theory began with the advent of the Big Bang Theory, particularly after Edwin Hubble's observations in the 1920s. Hubble, using a telescope, discovered something groundbreaking: all the celestial bodies in the universe—stars, galaxies, and planets—were moving away from each other. This was observed by looking at the redshift in the light from distant galaxies. When the spectrum of light shifts toward the red end, it indicates that the source of that light is moving away from the observer. From this observation, a simple and logical conclusion followed: if these celestial bodies are moving away from each other, then if we reverse time, there must have been a point when they were all together.

Imagine, for a moment, holding several balls in your hand and throwing them in different directions. As time passes, they will move farther apart. Now, it is only logical to say that if they are moving apart, they must have been together at some point in the past. This is a universal truth. In the same way, when scientists look at the universe, they conclude that it must have started from a single point, a singularity, where all matter and energy were concentrated. This point, they say, had infinite density and zero volume—this is the idea of "Creation Ex Nihilo," or the creation of something from nothing.

After the Big Bang, the universe began expanding and cooling. Scientists explain that if there had been even the slightest disturbance in the trillionth of a second after the Big Bang, the universe as we know it wouldn't exist. The fact that we are here today is the result of a delicate balance—a set of precise conditions, such as Earth's distance from the Sun, its gravitational force, speed, and many other factors, all tuned perfectly for life. These fine tunings are so precise that it's almost impossible to believe they occurred by chance. This is where the theory of the steady-state universe completely fell apart and the Big Bang theory became the prevailing explanation. The concept of "Creation Ex Nihilo" has now been proven—humanity and the universe were both created. The problem is, if we had believed the universe had always existed, and that humanity was eternal without a beginning or end, it would have been difficult to understand the purpose and nature of existence. Science has solved this for us. Yes, there was a creation. The question of whether there is a Creator or not often leads to various arguments.

To comprehend the intricate fine-tuning of the universe—such as the perfect structure of DNA—it requires immense intellect and collective effort. Despite our advanced intellect, humanity has only managed to uncover aspects of the natural world; we merely discover phenomena rather than create them. For instance, we have learned that the sun appears to rise in the east and set in the west due to the Earth's rotation. However, the sun neither rises nor sets—this is merely a physical phenomenon we have observed. Discovering this phenomenon does not mean we created the sun. Similarly, when a chick hatches from an egg after being kept warm for 22 days under a hen or in an incubator, the knowledge of this process does not equate to creating the chick. It is simply an understanding of how the process works. No matter how deeply we explore or how much information we gather, we are unlikely to find definitive evidence about the Creator through scientific discovery alone. Even the hen that lays the egg is unaware of the underlying mechanisms at play. Animals like crocodiles or elephants do not understand the qualities they are inherently equipped with, and humans themselves often struggle to grasp their full potential. Science continues to uncover these truths incrementally, but it is clear we are not the originators of these qualities. Perhaps, behind all this complexity, there exists a superior intelligence—a "mighty brain"—that has meticulously organized these phenomena. This idea is supported by mathematics and logic, which demonstrate that behind any organized system or intricate design, there must be a guiding intellect. Without such an intellect, the existence of such well-ordered systems would be difficult to explain.

In physics, the Second Law of Thermodynamics states that entropy—commonly understood as disorder—either remains constant or increases over time. For example, if a bomb explodes in a building, the structure is blown into pieces, scattering debris everywhere. No natural force on Earth can reassemble it into its original form without intervention. This is entropy: when a disturbance occurs, disorder increases. Bringing more people into a chaotic situation might maintain the same level of disorder or worsen it, but it will never restore order without deliberate effort.

Now consider the destroyed building. Humans can rebuild it, but this process requires a budget, intellect, and effort. The building doesn't reconstruct itself—it takes organized thought and action to restore order. This demonstrates a fundamental principle: to create order, a mind is required. To create disorder, no effort is needed. After disorder arises, restoring order demands intellect and deliberate intervention. Let's apply this principle to the Big Bang. A small explosion in everyday life never creates order; it amplifies chaos. Yet, the Big Bang, a massive cosmic event, allegedly led to the formation of an ordered universe with over 2 million known species on Earth. Studying even a single species in depth would take a lifetime, and yet we still wouldn't fully understand its behaviors, let alone how it came to exist. This is an endless exploration. So, the question arises: could such order and complexity emerge without the involvement of a supreme intelligence—a "mighty brain"?

Fred Hoyle, a renowned astronomer, once remarked that "the creation of man without a creator is a more complex phenomenon than claiming that a tornado sweeping through a junkyard could assemble a Boeing 747." Even the most skeptical person would find it absurd to believe that something as intricate as a Boeing 747 could form by chance. Hoyle used this analogy to illustrate how unlikely it is for something as complex as a human being to arise without intentional design. Richard Dawkins, in his book *The God Delusion*, addressed this argument. He quoted Hoyle's statement and responded with the chapter titled "The Ultimate Boeing 747". Dawkins argued that if humans are so complex that they require a creator, then the creator must be even more complex than humans. By this logic, Dawkins reasoned, the creator would also need a creator, leading to an infinite regress of creators. But this infinite regress misses a critical point. For the universe to exist, there must be a first cause—an uncaused Creator who is self-existent and doesn't require a creator. This being, often referred to as God, is the ultimate source of all existence. Without this uncreated Creator, the cycle of creators would stretch endlessly with no resolution. So, let's pause here and reflect. While we can debate the nature of the Creator, it's clear that the complexity and order we observe in the universe point to the existence of a higher intelligence—an uncaused, self-existent entity that requires no creator. This entity is the ultimate answer to the question of existence.

This brings us to the concept of a Creator described in the Qur'an, specifically in Surah Ikhlas (Chapter 112). It provides a profound definition of the Creator:

"He neither begets nor is born." (Qur'an 112:3)

At first glance, we often understand this verse as simply stating that God has no father or son. However, a deeper reflection reveals a far more significant meaning: "He Himself has not come out of anyone, nor has anyone come out of Him." This emphasizes God's eternal and self-existent nature—uncreated and unparalleled. This concept of the Creator being beyond human lineage or dependence resonates with the earlier discussion: for the universe and its intricate order to exist, there must be an eternal, uncaused being that stands outside the cycle of creation.

Further insight into this idea is provided in a Hadith from *Sahih Bukhari* (#3276). The Prophet Muhammad (peace be upon him) said:
"Satan comes to one of you and says, 'Who created such-and-such?' until he says, 'Who created your Lord?' So, when he inspires such a question, one

should seek refuge with Allah and abandon such thoughts."

This Hadith highlights a key point: while curiosity about creation is natural, there are questions that may lead to confusion or endless loops of speculation, such as asking who created the Creator. The Qur'an and Hadith emphasize that the Creator is eternal, self-sufficient, and unlike His creation—a concept that transcends human logic and comprehension. By understanding the definition provided in Surah Ikhlas and the guidance from this Hadith, it becomes clear that the Creator's existence is unique, independent, and beyond the scope of human limitations. In earlier times, discussions about the existence of God were limited by the knowledge and tools available. Now, with modern advancements in mathematical equations, scientific discoveries, and the universal truths that God has revealed to humanity, we have the means to delve deeper into these questions. These tools allow us to explain the existence of God with far greater precision and clarity. One critical concept is the fallacy of infinite regress: if the Creator had a creator, and that creator had another creator, this would lead to an endless cycle with no beginning. This is logically untenable because, for anything to exist, there must be a first cause—an uncaused Creator who initiated everything and exists independently. Now, you might ask, why should we believe in the existence of this one Supreme Being? The answer lies in the evidence all around us and in the principles of science and mathematics. Consider this: creation itself is an equation that proves its

Creator. If there were no creation, there would be no need to ponder a Creator. However, we observe the universe, its vast complexity, and its precise laws. From the fine-tuning of the cosmos to the structure of DNA, everything points to an intelligent design. If the universe were merely a theory without creation, we would have no reason to believe in a Creator. But creation is not theoretical—it is real. We see it, live it, and experience it. The intricate systems and harmony we observe cannot arise from randomness or chaos alone. Creation is the result of an equation with a solution: the Creator. Thus, we must view existence from a different perspective, one that acknowledges the evidence and logic of a singular, self-existent Creator. This Being is the uncaused cause, the One who has no creator, breaking the chain of infinite regress and grounding all reality.

Why God, Why?

When I look at the world around me, it's difficult to see what there is to be grateful for, especially when I feel as though I was placed on this earth without my consent. This world is full of trials, pain, and suffering. If God is all-loving, why would He allow this? Why does He let everyone suffer, and why does He threaten eternal damnation for those who fail to live up to His expectations? Even more puzzling is how He has prohibited so many of the things we find pleasurable in life. It's hard to fathom, especially when innocent people suffer. Every day, mothers die leaving behind infants. Every day, the innocent perish, while the guilty continue to live. How can this be? If I were to harm someone, I couldn't justify hurting the innocent—how could God, being all-loving, allow this? But then, I realized that these thoughts stem from human qualities I had mistakenly attributed to God. God is unseen, beyond our comprehension, independent of any system, and He is not bound by the limitations of time, space, or human understanding. He is the Creator, and His nature cannot be fully grasped by human minds. Why, then, did I imagine Him as if He were like us?

The Qur'an (21:23) makes it clear: "None shall question Him about what He does, but they shall be questioned." This means that the very question, "Why did You create me?" is not ours to ask in the way we think. Imagine, for a moment, If someone were thrown into a stormy sea, struggling to stay afloat, the immediate goal would be survival, not questioning who threw them in or why. The time to question would come only after reaching the shore, when there is clarity and safety. Similarly, our time on earth is our struggle to survive spiritually, and the answers to our deepest questions may not come until we reach the safety of the Hereafter. In the Hereafter, when we stand before God, our questions may seem irrelevant in light of the eternal rewards awaiting us. Human beings often prioritize short-term pleasures and pains over long-term benefits. The reality is that, in the grand scheme of eternity, the challenges and joys of this world are fleeting.

As the Prophet Muhammad (peace be upon him) said, "What is the parable of this worldly life, in comparison to the Hereafter, but one of you dipping his finger in the sea? Let him see what he brings forth." (Sahih Muslim 2858). This life, with all its ups and downs, is like a drop in the ocean compared to the infinite expanse of the Hereafter. We live for a few years, but God offers us the opportunity for eternal life.

This world can often seem like the final destination for many, but this perspective only emerges when we lose sight of the broader purpose of existence. If we view life purely as a finality, it leads us to misunderstand its true nature. However, if we understand life as a trial—an examination of character, choices, and actions—it begins to make sense. Human beings, by nature, tend to claim ownership over the world around them. People often say, "this is my money, my home, my family," but this sense of ownership is fleeting and ultimately illusory. What we truly "own" in a more lasting sense are the deeds we perform, not the material possessions we accumulate. The money we spend on necessities, the clothes we wear, and what we give in charity for the sake of the hereafter are the only possessions that are truly ours in an eternal sense. The rest is transient and remains behind, a legacy passed down to future generations.

A poignant illustration of this is the concept of "three friends" in life: wealth, family, and deeds. These three entities accompany us throughout our lives, but only one—our deeds—accompanies us into the grave. Wealth, family, and even our physical bodies remain behind, while only the sum of our actions follows us. This truth redefines what we consider important. It is the deeds we perform, the good we do, and the righteousness we uphold that will define us when our lives come to an end. Moreover, life is full of tests, and sometimes those tests involve encountering hardship or suffering at the hands of others. Often, bad people are given the opportunity to oppress good people, not because there is no justice, but because it serves as a test for the oppressed: will they remain patient, will they continue to do good despite their suffering? If life were only a path of garlands and easy success, what purpose would the hereafter serve?

When Allah created Paradise and Hell, He sent Jibril, peace be upon him, to Paradise and said: 'Look at it and at what I have prepared for its people in it.' He looked at it, then he came back and said: 'By Your Glory, no one will hear of it but he will enter it.' So He commanded that it be surrounded by hardships and said: 'Go and look at it and at what I have prepared for its people in it.' He looked at it and saw that it had been surrounded with hardships. He (Jibril) said: 'By Your Glory, I fear that no one will enter it.' He (Allah) said: 'Go and look at the Fire and at what I have prepared for its people in it.' So he looked at it and parts of it were piled upon other parts. He came back and said: 'By Your Glory, no one will enter it.' So He commanded that it be surrounded with pleasures and said: 'Go and look at it.' So he looked at it and saw that it was surrounded with pleasures. He came back and said: 'By Your Glory, I fear that no one will be saved from it and all will enter it.'" (Sunan an-Nasa'i 3763)

This powerful image shows that the divine wisdom behind the trials and temptations we face is not arbitrary. In the case of Paradise and Hell, Allah's test for humanity is a profound one, where those who endure hardship, resist temptation, and align their will with God's guidance are those who succeed in the Hereafter. The hardships we face are not random—they are divinely designed to sift through who will choose patience, perseverance, and righteousness, and who will succumb to the pleasures of this world, which lead to the eternal suffering of Hell. In this context, the reality of suffering and difficulty becomes clearer: it is part of the divine plan to purify us and guide us toward our true eternal home.

The hereafter is the space where true justice is enacted, where the scales of fairness are balanced, and where those who were wronged find their recompense. It is natural for humans to feel anger when wronged, and even to wish for justice to be done. When someone wrongs us, we may feel the urge to retaliate or wish that the wrongdoer experiences the same suffering. This inclination is not uncommon, but it is a reflection of our human weakness and limited understanding. While we may feel helpless to exact justice ourselves, we must remember that ultimate justice belongs to God. What may seem impossible for earthly courts to address—such as the atrocities committed during the Holocaust or the Mongol invasions—can be judged and rectified by God. No earthly court can provide adequate expiation for such heinous acts. If those dictators were to be somehow judged in a court, could the court sentence them as an expiation for the millions of people they killed? No, human courts are limited in their ability to provide justice for such heinous crimes. However, God can ultimately hold them accountable and provide true justice. God can sentence them a million times, and still, it would not be enough to atone for the immense suffering they inflicted.

This understanding of justice brings comfort, not because we avoid responsibility for our actions or ignore the pain of others, but because it assures us that all will be accounted for in the hereafter. The suffering of the innocent and the cruelty of oppressors are not forgotten; they are all part of the divine plan, and the scales of justice will be balanced in the most perfect way. In this sense, the suffering we endure in this world, though painful, is part of the trial, and the ultimate reckoning is something only God can perfectly enact. *"If anyone spends the night on the roof of a house with no stone palisade, Allah's responsibility to guard him no longer applies (Sunan Abi Dawud 5041)."*

For example If one chooses to wander the dangerous paths of night, alone and unaware, let them not cry out when the darkness swallows them. If you drink from the cup of recklessness, do not then seek to blame the winds for the storm that follows. The world is no kindly keeper; it rewards only those who engage with it fully, with purpose and foresight. Risk is a beast, but it is a beast tamed only by the strength of your own resolve. You must dare, you must act—and leave the rest to the hands of fate. But know this: effort is the law that governs this existence.

This Hadith underscores a profound truth: divine protection and justice are intertwined with human responsibility. If one neglects to secure the palisade—both literal and metaphorical—they step outside the bounds of divine guardianship. This serves as a reminder that God's protection is not a substitute for human effort but a complement to it. It is a call to align faith with preparation, trusting in divine justice while embracing personal accountability. Thus, the core of life lies not in wealth, possessions, or even family, but in the way we live our lives—how we treat others, the choices we make, and the good we contribute to the world. Our deeds will follow us, long after our wealth has dissipated, our bodies have decayed, and our families have moved on. Therefore, it is imperative that we focus not just on the temporary aspects of life, but on what truly matters in the eternal sense: our actions, our intentions, and our devotion to justice and goodness. In sum, the true nature of this world is not that it is the end of the journey, but that it is a temporary stage in a much larger cosmic test. Our role is to endure, to act justly, and to remember that ultimate justice and recompense belong to God alone. It is not for us to seek vengeance or retribution when we are wronged, but to trust in the perfect justice that awaits us in the hereafter.

Also the question of why an all-knowing God doesn't immediately place individuals in heaven or hell is a complex one, often raised as a challenge to the concept of divine justice and free will. To address this, we must consider the nature of human existence, the purpose of free will, and the role of suffering in moral development. Let's imagine, for a moment, that God did indeed act according to His omniscience and placed each person in their respective eternal destinations based solely on His knowledge of their actions and beliefs. Those destined for heaven might rejoice, but those destined for hell would undoubtedly raise the question, "Why are you condemning me to hell?" Even if God's decisions were entirely just, human nature, shaped by our experiences and emotions, would still compel us to ask for explanations when faced with hardship or suffering. It's a natural instinct to seek understanding when confronted with what we perceive as unjust.

This brings us to the crucial role of *free will* in the human experience. The gift of free will allows individuals to make choices, both good and bad, and this freedom is essential for moral growth and responsibility. If God were to predetermine each person's eternal fate, bypassing their personal decisions and moral development, the concept of free will would be meaningless. We would become mere puppets in a predetermined cosmic play, stripped of any genuine responsibility for our actions. Moreover, the existence of free will means that humans are ultimately responsible for their own fate. The potential for eternal separation from God—what some might interpret as hell—is not merely a result of divine punishment, but a consequence of one's own choices. It is through the exercise of free will, in which individuals choose to align or misalign with moral and divine principles, that they shape their own destiny. In this sense, one could argue that each person is, in a very real way, the "enemy" of themselves, as they have the power to choose paths that lead to their own ultimate suffering or salvation. Suffering, too, plays a critical role in this process. Human nature compels us to question why we experience pain, hardship, or failure. But rather than being merely an obstacle to be avoided, suffering serves as an opportunity for growth, reflection, and transformation. The decisions we make in the face of adversity, the way we respond to suffering, help to refine our character and align us more closely with our higher moral purpose. It is through grappling with the consequences of our actions that we come to understand the gravity of our choices, and ultimately, our responsibility in shaping our eternal future. Thus, the reason God doesn't immediately place us in heaven or hell is not a matter of arbitrary delay but of a profound respect for the autonomy of human beings. Our free will allows us to decide our destiny through the choices we make throughout our lives. Heaven and hell are not merely divine rewards and punishments, but the natural outcomes of how we choose to live, to love, and to act in relation to both others and the divine. The ultimate "enemy" we face is not an external force, but our own failure to recognize and embrace the responsibility we have over our actions and their consequences.

If you ask me which of God's qualities is beyond human understanding, I would say it is His eternal existence. We can imagine some of His attributes, like hearing and seeing, because we have an understanding of these things in our own limited, dependent way.

But God's qualities are different—His hearing and seeing are not limited in any way. His existence has no beginning or end. He has always been, and He will always be. This is something beyond human comprehension, something that cannot be fully explained. However, there is one aspect of God's nature that is more accessible to us: His promise of eternal life. While God's self-existence is a quality He alone possesses, He has promised to share with us the gift of eternal existence in Heaven, with the difference between Creator and creation. This is a profound gift—a chance to live forever in His presence, in a state of unimaginable peace and joy. If we earn that reward, we will experience a life beyond anything we can imagine.

This is the key to understanding why we should love God: He was, and is, alone in His eternal reign, and yet He has chosen to share a part of His eternal nature with us—He promises us eternal life in Heaven, a life that will far surpass anything we can experience on earth. This is the ultimate gift, and it is one that stems from His infinite love and mercy. In my reflections, I've coined the term "Mini-God" to capture the idea of our eternal nature as human beings—given to us by God, but with the eternal distinction between Creator and creation. We will never be like God, but through His mercy, we can share in a part of His eternal existence. The love of God grows within us when we realize that He, who had no obligation to do so, has chosen to share these eternal qualities with us. He offers us a life far greater than the fleeting pains and pleasures of this world. By focusing on this eternal perspective, we can begin to understand why we should love Him, even amidst the suffering and challenges of life.

SCHOLARS

In today's world, man has become a mere slave to the priest, the scholar, and the interpreter of holy doctrines. He submits his spirit to these self-proclaimed experts, trusting that their wisdom will lead him to the truth. But in doing so, he forfeits his own responsibility to grapple directly with the sacred texts, abandoning the raw power of personal engagement with the divine. These scholars are but intermediaries, and in their hands, the sacred words of the Creator are reduced to a mere spectacle, a commodity for intellectuals. Let us not forget: the true power of faith lies not in the hands of these so-called authorities, but in the texts themselves. It is only through confronting these writings directly, and without distortion, that we can claim the righteousness of our beliefs. Religion is not a passive inheritance handed down from one generation of scholars to the next. It is an active, fiery engagement with the divine that demands personal effort. Each individual must confront the sacred texts alone, untethered from the biases and interpretations of others. The texts speak for themselves. They are not mere words, but divine utterances, each line a doorway to profound wisdom. Only by confronting these words ourselves can we claim the truth they contain, free from the veil of distortion that clings to the interpretations of others.

This is the crux of the matter: we must not rely on others to interpret the text for us. The scholar, no matter how learned, is a fallible human being, bound by his own experiences, prejudices, and limitations. Even the most revered scholars are subject to misinterpretation. In their hands, the sacred texts may lose their purity, their unfiltered clarity. The true message is often buried beneath layers of thought and analysis, obscured by the scholar's own worldview. This is the danger of outsourcing our spiritual understanding: we relinquish our own power, and the teachings of the Creator become tainted.

History bears witness to this growing disconnection between man and his faith. Once, every individual had direct access to the sacred texts. They did not need the priest to decipher the words; the text itself was their guide, their companion. But over time, with the rise of literacy and the professionalization of religious scholarship, we allowed these experts to claim the right to interpret the sacred. And in doing so, we relinquished our direct connection to the divine, replacing it with a mediated, passive form of belief. Let us cast off this dependency. The scholar has his place, to be sure, but his place is not at the helm of our spiritual lives. We must reclaim that role for ourselves. The text, in its purest form, is the source of wisdom. And it is through a personal engagement with this source that we will find the truth we seek. The scholar may offer insight, but the text alone will guide us to the divine.

The greatest peril we face in our modern world is the loss of this direct engagement. To be a passive recipient of second-hand interpretations is to risk the distortion of the sacred message. The true path lies not in the hands of scholars, but in the individual's own struggle with the text, the direct confrontation with the teachings of the Creator. It is through this struggle that we will find clarity, understanding, and growth. Only by immersing ourselves in the texts can we avoid the error of misinterpretation and stay true to the essence of our faith. It is this direct engagement with the sacred that allows us to grow, to become not mere followers, but active seekers of truth. The scholar may offer guidance, but it is we who must interpret the text for ourselves, drawing out its wisdom and applying it to our own lives. Only through this active engagement can we avoid becoming mere vessels of interpretation, and instead become true vessels of the divine message.

In conclusion, the scholar has a role to play, but it is a limited role. It is not through the scholar that we find our faith, but through direct engagement with the sacred texts. We must take responsibility for our own spiritual understanding. The texts are there, waiting for us to open them, waiting for us to confront them directly. Let us not outsource our spiritual lives, but reclaim the power to interpret and understand the sacred for ourselves. In doing so, we ensure that we remain grounded in the truth, on the true path of righteousness, forged by our own understanding of the teachings that have stood the test of time.

Remember

The labyrinth of life—how inevitable it is that one
will stumble upon one's own lies and betrayals! For
what is man but a perpetual contradiction, a being
adrift between the poles of good and evil, pulled this
way and that by the tides of his own ignorance? Yet,
does he not rise after each fall? Does he not burn with
the fire of his own awareness, his sins transforming
into stepping stones, not barriers? If you would
change some things in your life, had you the chance to
live it again, that just means you have learned
something from life. To recognize the error, to see the
sin, to understand the ignorance—that is the gift of a
free spirit. One is forever walking the razor's edge of
self-deception. Do not fear the missteps, but rather the
failure to learn from them. For in the end, is not the
greatest victory to become the person who knows
when they have strayed and has the courage to turn,
not toward perfection, but toward becoming?

In every chaos, there is an order, although one might
not be able to see it on first try. The reason our lives
are different, why we feel varying emotions, face
challenges, perceive uniquely, and carry a nature
unlike any other, is what grants life its meaning. If we
were to be the same, what would we admire, ask for,
work for? Truly, sometimes being unaware is a
blessing, and sometimes it is a curse.

The self—what a curious thing! You claim to know
yourself, but who is this illusion that speaks of itself?
Is it not a mere role played for the eyes of others, a

mask worn to satisfy their gaze? The grandest of illusions—the "self" is but a mirage in the desert of your true desires. You think you are the man who does not need grand estates or the trappings of wealth—perhaps you are the simple soul, seeking only enough to sustain your spirit. But do not fool yourself: the self you think you know is as fragile and deceitful as the roles you cast yourself in. For the mind is but a servant to the world's impositions, never free to claim its own existence. In the crucible of struggle, I forged my path, solitary and unyielding. While you sought solace in each other's arms and squandered your strength in petty squabbles, I stood alone, unflinching before the storm, and faced all that life hurled my way. Behold now the fortitude I possess, wrought not by the mercy of others but by the fire of my own trials. And as for wishes or fulfilled desires—such indulgences are a fool's prize. What is freely given, offered without strife, is but a hollow gift, fleeting and devoid of essence, incapable of withstanding the test of eternity. Those fleeting gifts lack the authenticity of what one must fight for, carve out through suffering. It is only through the struggle, through the painful forging of one's spirit, that true desires are born—those desires which cannot be stolen, but are birthed from within. The law of nature: only the finest steel is carried by one, and even then, it's allowed to breathe, to stay alive. The greatest artisans have but one disciple, keeping their craft ever true to life's flame. True mastery is a rare gift, reserved for the few who have the strength to remain true, who do not succumb to the perversions of the world but craft their soul like the finest blade, tempered through trial and self-knowledge. In this, the world of contrast reveals its cruel wisdom: it is not through ease that one is forged, but through struggle. Only those who endure, who breathe life into their suffering, can begin to transcend the perpetual churn of existence. Do not be deceived: evolution may explain the natural world, but who dares claim it will teach you how to live? Nature's wisdom is indifferent to human vanity, indifferent to the hollow cry of "purpose." It is only through the clarity of one's own struggle, one's own suffering, that a man can begin to carve his path. The world remains indifferent—yet how often, in the darkest depths, do small acts of kindness from others have the power to strip away the fortress of selfishness we all tend to build? This is the paradox: it is through giving, not through taking, that we are made greater. Yet, do not forget that in a world of masks and roles, the true warrior is not defined by the shape of his body, but by the strength of his heart. He who stands firm in battle, in love, in life, does so because his heart is the weapon that guides him. And what of the fool? The one who makes a fool of himself in the face of beauty and grace—how often do we fall into the role of the jester for those we love? Should you not be that fool for yourself as well, embracing your eccentricities, unafraid to let your inner weirdo roam free? It is the moment we silence that strange, wild voice within that we betray our very essence, our very becoming. The hunger of man. The food that fills the hands of the homeless looks more precious, more vital, than it ever could in the hands of the rich. It is a law of nature: the less you have, the more you desire. And yet, the more you are given, the more hollow your desires become. The world operates not on equality, but on a grand trial of contrast. Those with much are tested in their ability to give, while those with little are tested by their endurance. And in the end, all are tested by their capacity to remain true to their own struggle, whatever form that may take.

Do you think that wealth is the ultimate trial? No, it is not in the possession of riches, but in the battle to remain unchanged by them. To remain the same—that is the true challenge, not to have wealth, but to not be consumed by it. For the mind must remain the master of the body, just as the heart must rule the mind. Only when you control your thoughts can you begin to control your life. Never let the third voice go unheard in your conversations, nor let the unseen child of the orphan be ignored. For what you love should never be shown in the shadow of another's pain. Here is the challenge: to not perpetuate the sickness of the world. So many are content to become mere actors on the stage of life, reciting lines they have not written, parroting ideologies they have not forged with their own hands. But you—yes, you—you must choose to speak truth, to refuse the role of the corrupted. The world is full of people who are content, yes, but what of those who truly live? To judge yourself truly is to measure yourself not against others, not against the expectations of the world, but against the ideal of who you could be, the highest version of your potential. Who are you when no one is watching, when all the masks are removed, when you stand alone before the abyss? Only then can you begin to see—only then do you confront the true self, the self that is not bound by the judgments of others, but is free, unshackled, ready to carve its own path in the cosmos.

Thus, do not wait for the moment of death to value life. No, value them now, these fleeting moments, for they will be gone before you know it. Cherish the tiny, fragile things—because one day, they will not be there. Imagine their absence now so that when they are gone, you can weep for what you had, not for what you missed. In the end, what is it to truly know yourself? Stand before the mirror of your own mind, and see who you truly are—not through the eyes of others, not through the perceptions of the world, but through the gaze of your deepest self. Only then, when you have reconciled the mirror of self with the perceptions of others and the distant, divine gaze of existence itself, can you begin to understand your place in the cosmic dance.

Conclusion

As I close these reflections on life, love, and humanity, I am struck by the great paradox of existence—the unity that binds us even as we stumble through its fragments. Each chapter of this work has been a thread, woven into the great tapestry of human striving, yearning, and becoming. It is not a neat picture, nor should it be. Life is no orderly canvas; it is a raw and tumultuous masterpiece, painted by the hands of God and mortals alike. At the heart of this journey stands the mother—a figure both eternal and fleeting, the quiet architect of our earliest virtues and vices. Her love is not a mere sentiment; it is a force of nature, relentless in its demands and transformative in its giving. She is the soil from which we grow, the shadow we cannot escape, and the foundation we dare not deny. To speak of a mother's love is to speak of the divine—raw, unadorned, and powerful beyond comprehension. And yet, even this love carries its own chains. It binds us, teaches us, and demands from us an answer to the ultimate question: What will you do with the life that was given to you? The family, too, is a crucible of paradox. A sanctuary, yes, but also a battlefield. Within its walls, strength clashes with vulnerability, rivalry with camaraderie. Fathers, siblings, and kin form a complex web of relationships, each strand vibrating with tension and affection. The family is not a place of simple peace—it is a forge where the soul is tested and tempered. And in its trials, we learn the greatest truths about ourselves. Beyond the family lies society, that grand theater of illusions. Modernity, with its dazzling lights and relentless pace, promises progress but delivers disconnection. Technology, that false prophet, claims to bring us closer while tearing apart the sacred bonds of presence and intimacy. We rush to embrace its gifts, only to find our hands empty. And yet, within this chaos lies a challenge worthy of the strongest wills: to reclaim the sacred, to see through the glittering veil of convenience and rediscover the timeless truths that ground us. Tradition and progress are locked in a ceaseless dance, their steps often stumbling but never ceasing. As the roles of men, women, and families shift, we must navigate this storm with courage and clarity. To discard tradition entirely is folly, for it holds the wisdom of countless generations. But to cling to it blindly is equally foolish, for progress is the very pulse of life. The challenge is to walk the razor's edge between the two, to honor the past while creating a future worthy of it. Ah, duality—how it haunts and exalts us. We are creators and destroyers, architects of beauty and engineers of ruin. Love itself is a battlefield, demanding that we lay bare our greatest strengths and deepest weaknesses. Freedom and responsibility are not opposites but companions, each incomplete without the other. To live is to struggle with these contradictions, to hold them in tension and find in them the essence of what it means to be human. And then there is death—the final horizon, the great leveling force. It casts its shadow over all we do, yet it is not an end but a beginning. Death compels us to see life for what it truly is: fleeting, fragile, and infinitely precious. It strips away illusions and demands urgency. Every moment becomes a question: Will you act, or will you waste the time given to you? In facing death, we do not despair; we awaken. Even in our darkest impulses—greed, power, exploitation—there lies the seed of redemption. History is not merely a tale of ruin but of resilience, a record of humanity's capacity to rise above its basest instincts. The will to power, so often misunderstood, is not a call to dominate but to create, to transcend the ordinary and reach for the extraordinary. Our flaws are not chains; they are the raw material from which greatness is forged. This book is not a set of answers but a challenge, a call to confront the sacred and the profane within ourselves. It is an invitation to step into the arena of life with open eyes and an unyielding spirit. What does it mean to love? To live? To leave a legacy that defies the void? These are the questions that demand not answers but action. Hope, that fragile and tenacious thing, is not a balm but a fire. It is the spark that compels us to rise, even when the weight of the world threatens to crush us. To hope is to refuse surrender, to believe in the possibility of beauty amidst chaos. It is not for the faint of heart, for hope requires strength—strength to see the world as it is and to strive to make it better. Hope prolongs human suffering said Nietzsche, yet in its very essence, it beats in harmony with it—a poignant paradox that both tortures and sustains us, for it is through this struggle that we find the will to endure, even as we are bound to the very pain we seek to escape. As I close this chapter, I do not offer comfort but a challenge: Embrace the contradictions, the struggles, the fleeting moments of joy and sorrow. Do not seek peace; seek greatness. Life is fleeting, but within its impermanence lies infinite potential. Let us seize it with ferocity and grace, with courage and compassion, knowing that in doing so, we honor the best of what it means to be human.